Twenty-One Modern Saints

*Biographies, Inspirational Words of Wisdom,
Confirmed Miracles, and
Final Resting Place*

Twenty-One Modern Saints

*Biographies, Inspirational Words of Wisdom,
Confirmed Miracles, and
Final Resting Place*

Robert Theophilus

LEONINE PUBLISHERS
PHOENIX, ARIZONA

Copyright © 2022 Robert Theophilus

All rights reserved. No part of this book may be reproduced or transmitted in any form or by any means, electronic or mechanical, including photocopying, recording, or by any information storage or retrieval system now existing or to be invented, without written permission from the respective copyright holder(s), except for the inclusion of brief quotations in a review.

Cover images, clockwise from top left: St. Teresa of Kolkata, St. Elizabeth of the Trinity, St. John Bosco, St. Óscar Romero, St. Joseph Moscati, and St. Josephine Bakhita.

Published by
Leonine Publishers LLC
Phoenix, Arizona, USA

ISBN-13: 978-1-942190-68-4

Library of Congress Control Number: 2022921396

Printed in the United States of America

10 9 8 7 6 5 4 3 2 1

Visit us online at www.leoninepublishers.com
For more information: info@leoninepublishers.com

Contents

Introduction 1

Chapter 1 3
St. Jean Vianney
1786-1859

Chapter 2 7
St. Teresa of Kolkata
1910-1997

Chapter 3 11
Saint Padre Pio
1887-1968

Chapter 4 16
St. Thérèse of Lisieux
1873-1897

Chapter 5 21
St. Elizabeth of the Trinity
1880-1906

Chapter 6 25
St. John Henry Newman

Chapter 7 30
St. Edith Stein
1891-1942

Chapter 8 35
St. John Bosco
1815-1889

Chapter 9 40
St. Elizabeth Ann Seton
1774-1821

Chapter 10 45
St. André Bessette CSC
1845-1937

Chapter 11 49
   BLESSED DINA BELANGER
   1897-1929

Chapter 12 53
   ST. DAMIEN DE VEUSTER
   1840-1889

Chapter 13 57
   ST. JOSEPHINE BAKHITA
   1869-1947

Chapter 14 61
   ST. MAXIMILLIAN KOLBE
   1894-1941

Chapter 15 65
   ST. FAUSTINA KOWALSKA
   1905-1938

Chapter 16 70
   ST. JOSEPH MOSCATI
   1880-1927

Chapter 17 75
   ST. KATHARINE DREXEL
   1858-1955

Chapter 18 79
   BL. JERZY POPIELUSZKO
   1947-1984

Chapter 19 83
   ST. FRANCES CABRINI
   1850-1917

Chapter 20 88
   ST. ÓSCAR ROMERO
   1917-1980

Chapter 21 93
   ST. GIANNA MOLLA
   1922-1962

Conclusion 97

Endnotes 99

Introduction

The title of this book is briefly *Twenty-One Modern Saints*. It will be useful to start out by defining what is meant by the word "saint." At its most basic level, a saint is any person who has died and whose soul is now in heaven with God. Only God knows who all of the saints are but there are some persons who lived lives of such outstanding holiness and such heroic virtue that the Church feels confident, after a sufficient examination, to declare that the person in question is a saint.

The process leading to canonization is usually lengthy and involved. The Catholic Church considers for sainthood people who were outstanding in holiness either because they died as witnesses for the faith (martyrs) or they lived a life of heroic virtue (confessors). When the official process leading to canonization, called a cause, is begun, the candidate receives the title Servant of God.

The second step toward canonization involves an examination of the documents supporting the candidate by the Congregation for Causes of Saints in Rome. If the evidence reveals true holiness, the pope is informed and he orders the Congregation to issue the Decree either of martyrdom or of heroic virtue, and the Servant of God is given the title Venerable. When the Servant of God has been declared a martyr, he or she may be beatified, that is, declared Blessed. If the Servant of God has been acknowledged to have lived a life of heroic virtue, it must be proven that one miracle has been granted by God through the intercession of the Venerable Servant of God. (Prior to the 1970s, two miracles were required.) Then, he or she is declared Blessed. The canonization of both martyrs and confessors requires one additional miracle, and it must be shown that this event took place through the intercession of the Blessed and after the date of his or her beatification.

The saints considered in this book are referred to as modern saints, inasmuch as they lived at least some of their life on earth during the 19th and/or 20th century. As a result, the Church has in her archives photographs of all but one of these saints and blesseds. Although most of the saints discussed here were members of the clergy or women religious, St. Joseph Moscati and St. Gianna Molla were lay persons. Also, the saints honored here came from a variety of backgrounds, including the dystopia of Auschwitz, the leper colonies of Molokai, the slums of Kolkata, and the killing fields of El Salvador.

It has been proposed that God grants miracles in response to the intercession of the saints in order to encourage us to imitate their holiness. It has been further suggested that one of the best ways to truly understand the meaning of scripture is to study the lives of the saints. The wisdom of the saints has also often influenced others for good. If you play with the light, you will also shine. Because true wisdom never has an expiration date or becomes "past tense," the saints' sterling words of advice have frequently been preserved for our edification. And this brings us to the major thrust of this book. The saints described herein were full of the Holy Spirit's gift of wisdom and it is the primary goal of this work to make this wisdom readily accessible in a single volume. May this same spirit teach us the fear of the Lord which is the beginning of wisdom.

Robert Theophilus
Solemnity of the Epiphany of the Lord
2021

CHAPTER 1

ST. JEAN VIANNEY
(LE CURÉ D'ARS)
1786-1859

Brief Biography

St. Jean Vianney resided in France from 1786-1859. He grew up on a farm during the terrors of the French Revolution, when the Vianney family sheltered many refugees and showed great charity toward the poor. At an early age, Jean felt a calling to the priesthood and so at age nineteen he entered the seminary, but the directors asked him to leave as they questioned his intelligence. A renowned priest friend convinced the seminary directors that Jean's great piety would make up for any perceived lack of intellect. He was ordained in 1815 and assigned to a parish in the small town of Ars. When he first arrived, the people were very negligent with regard to their faith and so Jean immediately arranged for catechism lessons. He was very dedicated to saving souls and he taught the faith without compromise. He also spent long hours in the confessional, lived a life of severe penance and, on occasion, healed the sick. As a result, he was often visited by demons who kept him awake at night with loud noises and who sometimes beat him.

With time, Jean became very famous and by 1855, twenty-thousand pilgrims, including priests, monks, nuns, and intellectuals, came every year to Ars to see and talk with him. In addition, he was often asked to preach in neighboring churches throughout the diocese. People began to recognize him as a saint and would cut off pieces of his cassock to keep as relics. Even the French government acknowledged Jean's contribution to the nation and appointed him Knight of the Imperial Order of the Legion of Honor. In spite of these tributes, and even when experiencing illness and old age, Jean continued to labor for the souls under his care. Finally, worn-out, he passed away on 4 August 1859. Out of respect, 300 priests attended his funeral. He was canonized in 1921 and declared to be the patron saint of parish priests. His body has remained incorrupt and can be seen in a glass reliquary in the Basilica of Ars.

Inspirational Words of Wisdom

- Do not do anything that you cannot offer to God.
- Offer your temptations for the conversion of sinners. Then the devil will leave, because the temptation is turned against himself.
- In the soul that is united to God, it is always springtime.
- Each of us is like a mirror in which God is searching for His reflection.
- Let us go to the foot of the Cross, we will learn there what God has done for us and what we ought to do for Him.
- God, in His goodness, has permitted us to speak to Him.
- When we give alms we should think that we are giving to the Lord and not to the poor.

- There is nothing easier than praying and nothing more comforting.
- We can, if we will, become a saint, for God will never refuse to help us to do so.
- Those who go to Mass during the week, often do their work much better than those who, for lack of faith, think they have no time for it.
- We are, in reality, only what we are in the eyes of God and nothing more.
- The Blessed Virgin loves above all to see in her children purity, humility, and charity.
- You must accept your cross; if you bear it courageously, it will carry you to heaven.
- There is nothing greater than the Eucharist. If God had something more precious, He would have given it to us.
- The Lord is more anxious to forgive our sins than a woman is to carry her baby out of a burning building.
- If you invoke the Blessed Virgin when you are tempted, she will come at once to your help and Satan will leave you.
- If people would do for God what they do for the world, what a great number of people would go to heaven.
- God commands you to pray, but forbids you to worry.
- Every consecrated host is meant to burn itself up with love in a human heart.

Confirmed Miracles

For Beatification

In September 1861, Adelaide Joly of Lyon was diagnosed as having a tumor in her arm. The prognosis was that she would always be crippled, with no hope of recovery. Together with the Daughters of Charity, she began a novena of prayers to St. Jean Vianney and at the end of the novena she was perfectly healed: the tumor had disappeared. The surprised doctors took notice of the healing and released a certificate, which was sent to the bishop of Belley.

The second miracle concerned Leo Roussat who suffered from epilepsy. In 1862 he experienced a violent attack and was carried to the grave of the late Curé. One of his arms hung crippled at his side, his power of speech was gone, and he experienced great difficulty in breathing. After a short time in prayer at the grave, he was taken back home. The hand, formerly crippled, was now able to give alms to the poor and he was able to walk again. At the conclusion of a novena, he was also able to speak with no further difficulty. On 8 January 1905, Pope Pius X declared Jean Marie Vianney Blessed.

For Canonization

At age twenty-eight, Marilde Rugeoi developed tuberculous of the larynx, with complete loss of her voice. Knowing that her illness was incurable, she went on a pilgrimage to Ars, where she kissed a relic of the holy Curé. Marilde, full of confidence in her heart, begged him: "If you want, you can heal me." Suddenly she started singing with the others—even though she had been mute for four years. The healing was instantaneous and complete. With a clear voice she made her depositions before the ecclesiastical court. Her recovery was a miracle.

CHAPTER 2

ST. TERESA OF KOLKATA
(MOTHER TERESA)
1910-1997

Brief Biography

Teresa was born Agnes Bojaxhiu on 26 August 1910 into a Kosovar Albanian family in Skopje under the Ottoman Empire. Teresa left home at age eighteen to join the Sisters of Loreto in Ireland to learn English in order to become a missionary. She was sent to India in 1929 and later took her solemn vows in May 1937 while she was a teacher at the Loreto convent school in Entally, eastern Kolkata. She served there for nearly twenty years and was appointed its headmistress in 1944. During a visit to Darjeeling, she heard an inner call to serve the poor of the city by living with them. In obedience, she left the school in 1948 and replaced her traditional Loreto habit with a simple, white cotton sari with a blue border. She obtained Indian citizenship, spent several months in Patna to receive basic medical training at Holy Family Hospital, and then ventured into the slums of Kolkata.

At the beginning of 1949, Teresa was joined by a group of young women who became the founding members of her Missionaries of Charity, a new religious community helping the "poorest among the poor." In 1952, Teresa opened her first hospice, converting an abandoned Hindu temple into the Kalighat Home for the Dying, subsequently renamed the Home of the Pure Heart (Nirmal Hriday). In 1979, Teresa received the Nobel Peace Prize "for work undertaken in the struggle to overcome poverty." On 13 March 1997, Teresa resigned as head of the Missionaries of Charity, and she died on 5 September of the same year. At the time of her death, the Missionaries of Charity had over 4,000 sisters operating 610 missions in 123 countries. These included hospices and homes for people with HIV/AIDS, leprosy and tuberculosis, soup kitchens, schools, and orphanages. Teresa was beatified on 19 October 2003, only six years after her death. She was canonized 4 September 2016. The body of Mother Teresa is located in the motherhouse of the Missionaries of Charity, 54A AJC Bose Road, Kolkata 700016, India.

Inspirational Words of Wisdom

- Here is the Gospel on five fingers: "You did it to me."[a]
- In the poor we nurse Him, feed Him, clothe Him, and visit Him.[b]
- We must be aware of our oneness with Christ. Our activity is truly apostolic only insofar as we permit Him to work in us and through us with His love.[c]
- Welfare is for a purpose, Christian love is for a person.[d]
- Take time to laugh; it is the music of the soul.[e]
- Take time to give; it is too short a day to be selfish.[e]
- Share what you have been given and that includes yourself.[f]
- Take whatever He gives and give whatever He takes with a big smile.[g]

- Let this sari remind me of my baptismal robe and keep my heart pure.[h]
- Spread love everywhere you go. Let no one ever come to you without leaving happier.[i]
- If you can't feed a hundred people, then feed just one.[j]
- Yesterday is gone. Tomorrow has not yet come. We have only today. Let us begin.[i]
- The most terrible poverty is loneliness, and the feeling of being unloved.[k]
- What can you do to promote world peace? Go home and love your family.[i]
- God doesn't require us to succeed, he only requires that we try.[i]
- Our progress in holiness depends on God and on ourselves—on God's grace and our will to be holy.[l]
- Love until it hurts.[m]
- All for Jesus.[n]

Confirmed Miracles

For Beatification

An Indian woman, Monica Besra, had a painful abdominal tumor that was so advanced her doctors abandoned all hope of saving her. The Missionaries of Charity decided to care for her and, on the first anniversary of Mother Teresa's passing, the sisters placed on Besra's stomach a Miraculous Medal that had been touched to the body of Mother Teresa. The suffering woman fell asleep, and when she woke up, her pain was gone.

Doctors examined her and found that the tumor had disappeared completely. Pope John Paul approved the miracle on December 20 2002, barely five years after Teresa's death.

For Canonization

In December 2008, Marcilio Andrino, a mechanical engineer from Santos, Brazil, had a bacterial infection in the brain that caused severe brain abscesses and agonizing head pain. A priest friend encouraged the young man and his wife, Fernanda Rocha, to pray for Mother Teresa's help. Andrino, however, slipped into a coma and while Rocha prayed, Andrino was taken for last-minute surgery. When the surgeon entered the operating room, however, he found Andrino awake. He made a full recovery, and went on to have two children, even though it was deemed by doctors to be a near medical impossibility. Father Kolodiejchuk, the postulator for the cause, referred to the children as a second miracle.

CHAPTER 3

SAINT PADRE PIO
(SAINT PIO OF PIETRELEINA)
1887-1968

Brief Biography

Padre Pio was born on 25 May 1887, in the village of Pietreleina in the south of Italy. He was later given the baptismal name Francesco (Franci). He began to experience apparitions and ecstasies at age five when he had resolved to consecrate himself to the Lord. In 1897, he met a Capuchin priest and decided that he also wanted to be a friar, and on 6 January 1903, he entered the Franciscan Friary at Marcone. He was given the name Brother Pio, and after six years of study he was ordained a priest. Through the rest of his life he experienced many mystical phenomena, including bilocation (being in two places at the same time), suffering the Lord's scourging every Thursday night, and being able to hear confessions in foreign languages that he otherwise did not understand.

On 4 September 1916, Padre Pio was assigned to the friary of Our Lady of Grace near San Giovanni Rotondo, and it was there that he received the stigmata. He bled from his wounds every day for the next fifty years. Once news of the stigmata became known, large numbers of people from all over the world came to his friary to assist in his Masses, confess to him, and just to see him. Padre Pio cared greatly about the physical as well as the spiritual well-being of his faithful. At his initiative and with the aid of many benefactors, he arranged for the construction of the Home for the Relief of Suffering, the largest hospital in the south of Italy, which opened on 5 May 1956. Shortly thereafter, Padre Pio himself became ill and after a prolonged period he was called home on 23 September 1968. He was beatified by Pope John Paul II on 2 May 1999, and canonized by the same Holy Father on 16 June 2002. St. Padre Pio's incorrupt body is in the sanctuary of St. Mary Our Lady of Grace, Piazzale Santa Maria delle Grazie, 71013 San Giovanni Rotondo FG, Italy.

Inspirational Words of Wisdom

- Pray, hope and don't worry. Worry is useless. Our Merciful Lord will listen to your prayer.[a]

- Prayer is the best weapon we have; it is the key to God's heart. You must speak to Jesus not only with your lips, but with your heart. In fact on certain occasions you should only speak to Him with your heart.[b]

- The life of a Christian is nothing but a perpetual struggle against self; there is no flowering of the soul to the beauty of its perfection except at the price of pain.[c]

- Walk in the way of the Lord with simplicity and do not torment your spirit. You must hate your defects but with a quiet hate, not troublesome and restless.[d]

- Have patience and persevere in the holy exercise of meditation; be content to begin with small steps 'til you have legs to run, better still wings to fly.[e]

- How can the mother of Jesus, present at the foot of the Cross on Calvary, who offered her Son as Victim for the salvation of souls, not be present at the mystical Calvary of the altar? ᶠ

- Have you not for some time loved the Lord? Do you not love him now? Do you not long to love him forever? Therefore, do not fear! Even conceded that you had committed all the sins of this world, Jesus repeats to you: "Many sins are forgiven thee because thou hast loved much!" ᵈ¹

- My past, O Lord, to your Mercy; my present, to your Love; my future, to your Providence! ᶜ¹

- If the soul would know the merit which one acquires in temptations suffered in patience and conquered, it would be tempted to say: Lord, send me temptations.ᵍ

- You must remember that you have in heaven, not only a Father but also a Mother… Let us then have recourse to Mary. She is all sweetness, mercy, goodness and love for us because she is our Mother. ᶠ¹

- Oh, how precious time is! Blessed are those who know how to make good use of it. Oh, if only all could understand how precious time is, undoubtedly everyone would do his best to spend it in a praiseworthy manner! ʰ

- In all the free time you have, once you have finished your duties of state, you should kneel down and pray the rosary. Pray the rosary before the Blessed Sacrament or before a crucifix. ⁱ

- It would be easier for the world to exist without the sun than without the Holy Mass. ʲ

Confirmed Miracles

For Beatification

On 31 October 1995, Consiglia De Martino from Salerno, Italy, noticed a growth in her neck that quickly reached the size of a grapefruit. After examination, her physician determined that her thoracic duct had ruptured, forming a huge lump of lymphatic fluid. Consiglia was told that she required a difficult and complicated surgery as soon as possible. She immediately phoned Padre Pio's monastery at San Giovanni Rotondo where she spoke with Fra Modestino Fucci—who, in turn, prayed at the tomb of Padre Pio on November 1 and 2. On November 2, Consiglia noticed a rapid diminution of the swelling in her neck. The following day she was examined by physicians and x-rays showed the complete cure of the rupture of the thoracic duct, the complete disappearance of the large two-quart liquid deposit in Consiglia's neck, and the complete disappearance of other liquid deposits in her abdomen. Evidently, Consiglia had been immediately and inexplicably cured of a dangerous medical condition—without any medical intervention whatsoever.

For Canonization

The miracle for canonization occurred at the Home for the Relief of Suffering located a few steps from Padre Pio's tomb. On the morning of 20 January 2000, seven-year-old Matteo Colella was seized with high fever, weakness, headache, vomiting, and mental disorientation. He was taken to the Home for the Relief of Suffering where he went into a coma and the prognosis was that he would soon die. Matteo's mother went to pray at Padre Pio's tomb, and soon after the boy woke up. The mother questioned him if he remembered anything. "Yes, I saw an old man with a white beard and a long brown habit. He gave me his right hand and said: "Matteo, don't worry, you will get well quickly." The mother showed him a picture of Padre Pio, and the boy identified him as the old man he had seen. A CAT scan did not reveal any kind of lesion in Matteo's brain, and on February 6, he left the hospital completely healed.

CHAPTER 4

ST. THÉRÈSE OF LISIEUX
(ST. THÉRÈSE OF THE CHILD JESUS AND OF THE HOLY FACE)
1873-1897

Brief Biography

Thérèse of the Child Jesus is one of the most famous saints of the Church. There are those who become saints by living lives of heroic virtue, and then there are those, like St. Thérèse, who become saints because they were called by God at an early age to accomplish some specific mission for the benefit of the Church. Thérèse lived during the second half of the 19th century and entered the Carmel of Lisieux when she was only fifteen. Almost immediately she experienced the dark night of the soul, which is a sharing of Christ's feeling of abandonment on the Cross. She often said that God was leading her by a subterranean way where there is no light, only darkness.

At age twenty-four, near the end of her life on earth, the mother superior of her convent asked Thérèse to write an account of her life. In obedience, Thérèse wrote her autobiography, which she called simply *The Story of a Soul*, and it was here that she described her little way of spiritual childhood. About this time she also contracted tuberculosis, which spread throughout her body and caused her great suffering. Prior to her death, she told her Carmelite sisters that they would not have time to miss her as the postman would keep them very busy on her account. In prophesying the number of miracles that would be performed at her intercession, she said: "You will see, it will be like a shower of roses." Sister Thérèse passed away on 30 September 1897. Upon the death of one of their community, it is the custom of Carmel to publish a short account of the sister's life and send it to other Carmelite convents. In the case of Sister Thérèse, it was decided that *The Story of a Soul* would serve the purpose. The book first appeared in 1898, and immediately it met with an enthusiastic reception. From convent to convent it was read with alacrity, and from the convents it was lent to others. By 1932 the circulation had risen to over two million copies, and it has since been translated into thirty-five languages. Upon reading the book, people began to ask Sister Thérèse for her intercession, and thus began the promised shower of roses. From every part of the world there were reports of miracles such that by the 1930s over a thousand letters a day were arriving at the Carmel of Lisieux. Obviously, this holy and brave daughter of Normandy was fulfilling her pledge to keep her sisters too busy to miss her. Some of her early biographers have referred to her as a Storm of Glory. She was canonized by Pope Pius XI on 17 May 1925. The relics of St. Thérèse are located at the Carmel of Lisieux, 37 Rue du Carmel, 14100 Lisieux, France, and the Basilica of St. Thérèse, 1 Avenue John XXIII, 14100 Lisieux, France.

Inspirational Words of Wisdom

- My final vocation is love. In the heart of my mother the Church, I shall be love.
- It is for us to console our Lord, not for Him to be always consoling us.

- We must give without counting the cost, practice the virtues, conquer ourselves and prove our love by every sort of tenderness and loving attention.
- Let us make our heart a little garden of delight where Jesus can come to find rest.
- My Jesus, you know full well that I do not serve you for your reward, but solely because I love you.
- What matters is that God wishes to be loved and must be loved.
- How can He be outdone in generosity?
- Now I know that true charity consists of bearing all my neighbor's defects, in not being surprised by mistakes, and being edified by the smallest virtues.
- From my earliest days I have believed that the little flower would be plucked in the springtime of her life. But today my only guide is self-abandonment. I no longer know how to ask passionately for anything except that the will of God should be accomplished perfectly in my soul.
- Instead of being discouraged, I told myself that God would not make me wish for something impossible so, in spite of my littleness, I can aim at being a saint.
- Abide in me as you abide in the tabernacle.
- It is impossible to describe the secrets of heaven in the words of earth.
- Do not be troubled, Mother, if I suffer a great deal and if I show no sign of happiness at the last moment. Did not our Lord die a victim of love and see what agony He had.

Confirmed Miracles

For Beatification

Sister Louise of St. Germain had suffered with stomach ulcers from 1913 to 1916. On 10 September 1916, she prayed to St. Thèrése who subsequently appeared to Sister Louise and said: "Be generous, you will recover soon, I promise you." In the morning, several nuns found rose petals strewn around the bed of the patient. A few days later, on September 22, Sister Louise awoke fully healed. Supporting the treating doctor's certificate are a conclusive x-ray and two reports—one from the eminent Dr. Bec, a Surgeon at St. Joseph Hospital in Paris, and another one from Dr. Victor Pauchet, a highly recognized doctor—confirming the supernatural nature of this sudden and sustainable transformation.

The second cure involved Charles Anne, a twenty-three-year-old seminarian who was dying from advanced pulmonary tuberculosis. The night he thought he was dying, Charles prayed to Thérèse. Afterward, the examining doctor testified, "The destroyed and ravaged lungs had been replaced by new lungs, carrying out their normal functions and about to revive the entire organism. A slight emaciation persists, which will disappear within a few days under a regularly assimilated diet."

For Canonization

Once she was declared Blessed, it took only two years for the necessary next two miracles to be approved. In 1925, two cures had been investigated and judged to be supernatural, through the intercession of St. Thérèse.

The first involved Sister Gabrielle Trimusi from the Convent of the Poor Daughters of the Sacred Heart in Parma, Italy. Gabrielle had suffered from arthritis of the knee and tubercular lesions on the vertebrae. All remedies proved ineffective, so she was counseled by a priest on 13 June 1923, to participate in a public novena in honor of Blessed Thérèse. After the novena, she took off the apparatus she wore to support the spine, and cried out loudly: "I am cured, I am cured!" Sister Gabriella Trimusi returned at once to her labors and the exercises of religious life, without either pain or fatigue. The doctors appointed by the Sacred Congregation concluded that she was healed by a miracle.

The final cure involved Maria Pellemans of Schaerbeck, Belgium. Maria suffered from pulmonary tuberculosis, which had spread, as Thérèse's illness had, to the intestines. The diagnosis of pulmonary and intestinal tuberculosis was made by a Dr. Vandensteene, who also examined Maria after she came back from praying at St. Thérèse's grave. The doctor testified, "I found Miss Pellemans literally transformed. This young woman, out of breath from the least movement, moves about without fatigue; she eats everything given to her, with a very good appetite. The abdomen presents no tender point, when formerly the least pressure produced severe pain. All symptoms of tubercular ulceration of the intestine have disappeared."

CHAPTER 5

ST. ELIZABETH OF THE TRINITY
1880-1906

Brief Biography

Elizabeth of the Trinity was born in 1880 in Avord, France, and later moved to Dijon where she grew up in close proximity to Dijon's Carmelite monastery. As a teenager she was a gifted pianist and enjoyed going to parties and other social events. During her first visit to the Dijon Carmel, the prioress informed her that her Christian name meant House of God. Elizabeth was very inspired by this fact and resolved that she would try to live a more Godly and disciplined life.

When Elizabeth revisited the monastery at age seventeen, the mother superior said, "I just received this circular about the death of Thérèse of Lisieux, and I want you to read it." The circular was, in fact, the first edition of St. Thérèse's *The Story of a Soul*, and when Elizabeth read it she knew she needed to become a Carmelite. She entered the Carmel in Dijon in 1901 and became an exemplary sister. While in Carmel, Elizabeth wrote several works including her prayer: "O My God, Trinity Whom I Adore." The spiritual missions of Thérèse of Lisieux and Elizabeth of the Trinity coincide, and the great theologian Hans Urs von Balthasar recognized that in his book *Two Sisters in the Spirit*. Elizabeth passed away in 1906 in great suffering from Addison's disease. Her last words were: "I am going to Light, to Love, to Life."

Elizabeth of the Trinity was canonized by Pope Francis on 26 October 2016. Her reliquary is located in St. Michael's Catholic Church, 5 Place Saint-Michel, 21000 Dijon, France.

Inspirational Words of Wisdom

- The horizons of Carmel are much more beautiful. There is nothing left here except Him and He is everything.
- How can I imitate in the heaven of my soul, the unceasing adoration of the saints in heaven's glory.
- We carry our heaven within us since He who completely satisfies the glorified saints in the full light of vision is the same one who gives Himself to us in faith and mystery. I feel as if I have found my heaven on earth because heaven is God and God is living within me.
- A praise of glory is someone who lives in God, who loves Him purely and unselfishly, not looking for any sweetness for herself, she loves Him above all His gifts and would love Him even if she received nothing.
- A praise of glory is someone who is always giving thanks; everything she does or thinks or dreams plunges her more deeply into love and is like an echo of the eternal Sanctus.
- Even if you grieve Him, remember that deep calls to deep; that the depths of your wretchedness calls to the depths of His mercy.
- Try to find your joy not in feelings but in the will.

- That I might walk the way of the cross as bride of the crucified.
- "Because I love My Father, I do always the things that are pleasing to Him." Thus spoke our holy Master, and every soul who wants to live close to Him must also live this maxim. The divine good pleasure must be its food, its daily bread; it must let itself be immolated by all the Father's wishes in the likeness of His adored Christ.
- I pray that the Master reveal to you His divine presence. It is so pleasant and sweet, it gives so much strength to the soul; to believe that God loves us to the point of living within us, to become the companion of our exile, our confidant, our friend at every moment.
- During painful times, when you feel a terrible void, think about how God is enlarging the capacity of your soul so that it can receive Him.
- May the Word imprint His beauty within you so that He can see Himself in you. May the Holy Spirit who is Love make of your heart a burning fire which will give joy to the three divine Persons by the heat of its flames.
- Always believe in love, in the radiant triumph of love.

Confirmed Miracles

For Beatification

Cardinal Albert Decourtray, the bishop of Dijon from 1974 to 1981, was cured of cancer through the intercession of Elizabeth. This miracle was accepted for her beatification in 1984.

For Canonization

In 2002, Marie-Paul Stevens, a Belgian woman who had Sjögren's syndrome, asked Bl. Elizabeth to help her manage the extreme pain of her disease. Because she felt like she had received graces, she traveled to the Carmelite monastery just outside Dijon to give thanks, and when she got to the monastery she was completely healed.

CHAPTER 6

ST. JOHN HENRY NEWMAN
1801-1890

Brief Biography

John Henry Newman was born in England on 21 February 1801, and lived almost the entire 19th century. After an early education at Ealing, he was accepted at Trinity College, Oxford, when he was only sixteen. In 1822, when he was just twenty-one, he was elected a fellow of Oriel College, then the center of academic excellence. In 1825, he was ordained a minister of the Church of England and in 1828 he was made vicar of University Church St. Mary the Virgin, a position of considerable influence. In 1833, he became very ill and vowed to work to renew the Church of England and thus began the famous Oxford movement. As time went by, the tracts published by the movement became more and more Catholic in content and Newman eventually resigned from his position at Oxford and went to live in Littlemore as a layman. It was at this time that he wrote "An Essay on the Development of Christian Doctrine," and in doing so, wrote himself out of the Anglican Communion.

On 9 October 1845, he was received into the Catholic Church, and in 1847 he was ordained a Catholic priest. Newman then joined the Congregation of the Oratory and later established a chapter in the city of Birmingham. He subsequently faced much opposition and derision from both within and outside of the Church, although he also had a number of friends who supported and consoled him. It was during this period that he wrote two of his most famous works: "An Essay in Aid of a Grammar of Assent" and the *Apologia Pro Vita Sua* (a defense of his life). In the end, Newman was vindicated and, when he was seventy-eight years old, Pope Leo XIII called him to Rome and made him a cardinal. He returned to England to a series of grand receptions in both London and Oxford. On 11 August 1890, at age eighty-nine, he passed away. His reputation, however, lived on, and the Second Vatican Council was often referred to as Newman's Council. Cardinal Newman is buried in the cemetery at Rednal Hill, Birmingham, at the country house of the oratory.

Inspirational Words of Wisdom

- God has created me to do Him some definite service; He has committed some work to me that He has not committed to another. I have my mission—I may never know it in this life, but I shall be told it in the next. He has not created me for naught, I shall do good, I shall do His work; I shall be an angel of peace, a preacher of truth in my own place, while not intending it, if I do but keep His commandments and serve Him in my calling. Therefore I will trust Him. If I am in sickness, my sickness may serve Him; in perplexity, my perplexity may well serve Him; if I am in sorrow, my sorrow may serve Him. He does nothing in vain. He may prolong my life; He may shorten it; He knows what He is about.

- Jesus is the Light of the world illuminating everyone who comes into it, opening our eyes with the gift of faith, making souls luminous by His almighty grace, and Mary is the Star, shining with the light of Jesus, fair as the moon and special as the sun; the star of the sea, which is welcome to the tempest-tossed, at whose smile the evil spirit flies and peace is poured upon the soul.

- I sought to hear the voice of God and climbed the topmost steeple, but God declared: "Go down again—I dwell among the people."
- Good is never accomplished except at the cost of those who do it, truth never breaks through except through the sacrifice of those who spread it.
- With Christians, a poetical view of things is a duty. We are to see a divine meaning in every event.
- To be deep in history is to cease to be a Protestant.
- A cloud of incense was rising on high; the people suddenly all bowed low; what could it mean? The truth flashed on him, fearfully yet sweetly; it was the Blessed Sacrament—it was the Lord Incarnate who was on the altar, who had come to visit and bless His people. It was the Great Presence, which makes a Catholic Church different from every other place in the world; which makes it, as no other place can be—holy.
- Ten thousand difficulties do not make one doubt, as I understand the subject; difficulty and doubt are incommensurate.
- Providence has delivered me of every worldly passion, save this one; the desire to acquire books, new or old books of any kind, whose charms I cannot persuade myself to resist.
- Fear not that thy life shall come to an end, but rather fear that it shall never have a beginning.

- Lead kindly Light amid the encircling gloom.
  Lead Thou me on.
  The night is dark and I am far from home, Lead Thou me on,
  Keep Thou my feet; I do not ask to see
  The distant scene; one step enough for me.
- *Cor ad cor loquitur:* heart speaks unto heart.
- May He support us all the day long, till the shades lengthen, and the evening comes, and the busy world is hushed, and the fever of life is over, and our work is done. Then in His mercy may He give us a safe lodging, and a holy rest, and peace at last.

Confirmed Miracles

For Beatification

Jack Sullivan had undergone spinal surgery because his lumbar vertebrae and discs were squeezing his spinal cord. During the procedure the surgeons encountered serious complications and days later he was still afflicted with a serious spinal condition, causing intolerable pain with no prospect of relief. One surgeon even told him that he was on the brink of complete paralysis! Jack could barely move and could not see how he could complete his studies to become a deacon for the Archdiocese of Boston. He called upon his special intercessor Cardinal John Henry Newman, praying: "Please, Cardinal Newman, help me to walk, so that I can return to classes and be ordained." As soon as he had completed this prayer, he felt a sensation of intense heat all over, which seemed to last a long time! In addition, he felt an indescribable sense of joy and peace, as though in the presence of God. When this moment subsided, he realized, that he had no more pain, whereas minutes before, he was bent over in agony. He could walk with strength in his back and legs! He was discharged, and to everyone's astonishment he returned to his classes on time. Cardinal Newman was beatified by Pope Benedict XVI on 19 September 2010, in his home city of Birmington.

For Canonization

Melissa Villalobos, a mother of four children who had a strong devotion to Bl. John Henry Newman, started bleeding during the first trimester of a pregnancy in 2013. An ultrasound revealed that there was a hole in the placenta that was allowing blood to escape. The doctors recommended bed rest. One subsequent morning she woke up in bed in a pool of blood. She put off calling 911 because she didn't know who would care for her children if she was taken in an ambulance. The bleeding intensified and she collapsed on the bathroom floor. With thoughts of losing her unborn baby, worry for her other children, and wondering if she could die, Villalobos uttered her fateful prayer to Cardinal Newman to make the bleeding stop. As soon as she finished the sentence, the bleeding stopped. She thanked Cardinal Newman and just then the scent of roses filled the bathroom. She got off the floor and verified there was no more bleeding. That afternoon, Villalobos' cure was confirmed during a weekly ultrasound. The doctor told her everything was "perfect," and there was no longer a hole in the placenta. The miracle was accepted by the Vatican and Cardinal Newman was canonized by Pope Francis on 13 October 2019.

CHAPTER 7

ST. EDITH STEIN
(ST. TERESA BENEDICTA OF THE CROSS)
1891-1942

Brief Biography

Edith Stein was born 12 October 1891, in Breslau, Germany (now Wroclaw, Poland). From the time Edith was a young girl, she worked hard and excelled throughout her school years. She was always loving and kind, but in her senior years at college she considered herself an atheist. At university, she entered the School of Philosophy and eventually became the student and friend of the famous philosopher Edmund Husserl. She attended some lectures by Max Scheler and, of these, Edith wrote: "He propagated Catholic ideas with all the brilliance of his intellect. This was a contact with a world that was previously unknown to me and one which I could no longer ignore." During the First World War, Professor Reinach, a Catholic convert, was killed at the front line and so his wife asked Edith to come and arrange her husband's philosophy papers. Edith wrote: "It was then that I first encountered the cross and the divine strength it gives to those who have to bear it. For the first time I saw before my eyes the Church, born of Christ's redemptive suffering, victorious over the sting of death. It was the moment that my unbelief collapsed."

Soon after, Edith had the opportunity to read the life of St. Teresa of Avila, and on finishing it she exclaimed: "This is the truth." She bought a catechism, read it, and then immediately sought baptism. On 1 January 1922, Edith was received into the Church and chose as her baptismal name, Teresa. She went from being a professor of philosophy to being an instructor at a Catholic girls' school. However, this gave her time to study St. Thomas Aquinas and her subsequent writings on St. Thomas made such an impact on the Catholic world that she won a new fame as a Catholic writer and speaker. Thus she spent the next five years, while longing to give herself to Christ as a Carmelite. Her spiritual advisor, however, urged her to continue to use her great talents for the glory of God. By the mid-1930s, she began to ask Jesus to allow her to offer herself as an oblation for the salvation of the Jewish people. The Nazis soon ordered that Dr. Stein must discontinue her teaching, so on 15 April 1934, Edith finally became a bride of Christ. By now the Nazis were attacking both Jews and converts and Edith (Sister Teresa Benedicta of the Cross) was secretly transferred to the convent in Echt, Holland. In August 1942, Edith was arrested by the Gestapo and sent to the Auschwitz concentration camp where she died in the gas chamber. Her body was likely cremated.

Inspirational Words of Wisdom

- God is love and love is goodness giving itself away. It is a fullness of being that does not want to remain enclosed in itself, but rather to share itself with others, to give itself to them and to make them happy. All of creation exists thanks to this divine love spending itself.[a]

- When the attraction to religious life awakens in the soul, it is as if the Lord were courting her. And if she consecrates herself to Him by profession of the vows and harkens to the "Come spouse of Christ," it is like an anticipation of the heavenly marriage feast.[b]

- On the question of relating to our fellow man— our neighbor's spiritual need transcends every commandment. Everything else we do is a means to an end. But love is an end already, since God is love.[c]

- The limitless loving devotion to God, and the gift God makes of Himself to you, are the highest elevation of which the heart is capable; it is the highest degree of prayer. The souls that have reached this point are truly the heart of the Church.[d]

- Since Mary is the prototype of pure womanhood, the imitation of Mary must be the goal of girls' education.[e]

- Every true prayer is a prayer of the Church; by means of that prayer the Church prays, since it is the Holy Spirit living in the Church, who in every single soul, "prays in us with unspeakable sighs."[a1]

- If anyone comes to me, I want to lead them to Him.[f]

- Both spiritual companionship and spiritual motherliness are not limited to the physical wife and mother relationship, but they extend to all people with whom woman comes into contact.[g]

- Learn from Saint Thérèse to depend on God alone and serve Him with a wholly pure and detached heart. Then, like her, you will be able to say, "I do not regret that I have given myself up to Love."[h]

- Those who join the Carmelite Order are not lost to their near and dear ones, but have been won for them, because it is our vocation to intercede to God for everyone.[i]

- Usually one gets a heavier cross when one attempts to get rid of an old one.[j]
- The motive, principle, and end of the religious life is to make an absolute gift of self to God in a self-forgetting love, to end one's own life in order to make room for God's life.[k]
- Anyone who seeks truth seeks God, whether or not he realizes it.[c]
- Many a dead person lies there after the fight like a victor, in majestic calm and deep peace. Could the simple cessation of life bring forth such an impression? And could it be thought that the spirit, which has impressed this seal on the body, does not exist anymore?[l]
- Do not accept anything as love which lacks truth.[m]

Confirmed Miracles

For Beatification

Edith Stein was beatified as a martyr on 1 May 1987. Consequently, no miracle was required.

For Canonization

In 1987, when Benedicta McCarthy was two, her parents left her at her home with her eleven older siblings, and she found and swallowed sixteen lethal doses of Tylenol. Benedicta's parents, arriving home, learned that their little daughter was in a coma with her liver and kidneys failing. The McCarthy family asked everyone they knew to begin praying to Edith Stein to intercede with God to save Benedicta's life. This chain of people praying to Edith Stein spread across the country. Within days, Benedicta walked out of the hospital totally recovered, carrying a red balloon. "I'm not saying it was a miracle," said Dr. Ronald Kleinman, who treated her at Massachusetts General Hospital, in a subsequent interview. "I'm Jewish. I don't believe per se in miracles, but I can say I didn't expect her to recover." Pope John Paul II canonized Edith Stein on 11 October 1998, in Vatican City.

CHAPTER 8

ST. JOHN BOSCO
1815-1889

Brief Biography

John Bosco was born on 16 August 1815, in Becchi in the Piedmont region of Italy. He was raised on a subsistence farm by a very pious mother and at a young age decided he wanted to become a priest. In 1835, with the financial aid of others, he entered the seminary, and in 1841 he was ordained. He began his ministry in Turin, where boys were coming to find work in the construction industry. Many of these boys survived in squalor by stealing, while others, as young as eight years old, had to do very heavy construction work. One morning a ragged fifteen-year-old bricklayer named Bartholomew Garelli entered the sacristy, and when Don Bosco offered to teach him catechism, the boy agreed. The next Sunday he returned with six other ragged boys and by the Feast of the Annunciation there were twenty-five more. Their religious instruction was enlivened by games and became so popular that soon there were over 100 boys. Wherever Father Bosco went, his group of boys, which he called the Oratory of St. Francis de Sales (the Salesians), came with him.

They finally found a permanent home in an old shed attached to a broken-down house in the middle of a damp and muddy field. The shed was soon turned into a chapel and a classroom, and Don Bosco gradually rented more sheds and rooms nearby, which he also turned into work and study rooms. He began to instruct the boys in trades such as tailoring and carpentry and to give evening classes in languages and geography. He subsequently built up a wide circle of friends and benefactors who helped to support his work. For a while Father Bosco became very ill with pneumonia, and on recovering his mother joined him to help care for his boys. Don Bosco also gave the members of his oratory spiritual talks, taught them to pray, heard their confessions, and encouraged devotion to Our Lady Helper of Christians. When away from the Oratory, he often suffered physical attacks and persecutions until a large dog appeared and for the next thirty years protected him. Don Bosco also worked many miracles, including restoring sight to the blind and helping a paralytic to walk again. His Salesians eventually became a religious order, and today there are missionaries of Don Bosco working with street children in almost every country of the world. On 31 January 1889, completely worn out from his labors, Don Bosco went to his reward in heaven. The body of St. John Bosco is in a reliquary in the Basilica of Our Lady Helper of Christians in Turin, Italy.

Inspirational Words of Wisdom

- Give me only souls and keep the rest.
- Do not try to excuse your faults; try to correct them.
- Enjoy yourself as much as you like, just keep from sin.
- Do not put off until tomorrow the good you can do today. You may not have a tomorrow.
- My life experience has been that only the practice of religion can assure concord in families and the happiness of those who live in this valley of tears.
- Be brave and try to detach your heart from worldly things. Do your utmost to banish darkness from

your mind and come to understand what true, selfless piety is.

- Health is God's great gift and we should spend it entirely for Him. Our entire body should serve God while we still have the time. Then when He shall take our health and we shall near our last, our conscience will not reproach us for having misused it.
- Guard your eyes since they are the windows through which sin enters the soul.
- There are plenty of ways to practice mortification! Just patiently endure cold, heat, sickness, troubles, people, happenings, and so forth.
- Fly from bad companions as from the bite of a snake.
- Only God knows the good that can come about by reading one good Catholic book.
- Willingly suffer a bit for God Who suffered so much for you.
- Jesus longs to grant you favors, especially those you need for your soul.
- The principal trap that the devil sets for young people is idleness.
- Be good, that will make your angel happy. When sorrows and misfortunes afflict you, turn to your guardian angel with strong trust and he will help you.
- Ask your angel to assist you in your last moments.
- I am leaving you here on earth, but only for a short while. Let us hope that through God's infinite

goodness, we shall all meet again one day in Eternity. I shall wait for you there.

Confirmed Miracles

For Beatification

In 1905, Sister Provina Negro, a daughter of Mary Help of Christians (the woman's religious order started by John Bosco), developed a hemorrhaging stomach ulcer. Her condition became increasingly serious and each attempted remedy failed. Sister Provina decided to pray a novena to Don Bosco and then she decided to go even further. She swallowed an image of Don Bosco, and from that moment she felt perfectly healed; all illness ceased forever. The doctors of the Congregation of Rites were all in agreement that the cure was to be attributed to supernatural forces.

The second miracle concerned a Miss Teresa Callegari of Castel San Giovanni. She had been ill with chronic arthritis and a combination of other disorders affecting vital organs and had been continuously bedridden. In January 1921, at twenty-six years of age, she prayed a first novena to Don Bosco with no results. One morning during a second novena, she had a vision of Don Bosco advancing toward her bed and ordering her to get up, and she soon discovered that she was cured. Don Bosco was beatified by Pope Pius XI on 2 June 1929.

For Canonization

For twenty-eight years, Mrs. Catherine Lanfranchi Pilenga suffered from chronic arthritic diathesis that practically paralyzed her lower limbs. In May 1931, she went to Turin and went to the Church of Mary Help of Christians where she sat down to pray in front of the urn that contained the mortal remains of Don Bosco. At some point deep in prayer, she knelt down. After remaining on her knees about twenty minutes, she stood up, walked to the altar of the Blessed Virgin, and knelt again to continue her prayers. It was only then that she suddenly realized that in kneeling, she was doing something impossible for her—and knew she was cured. Her disease had simply vanished. It was an instantaneous, total, and permanent recovery, verified by three doctors as well as a medical commission appointed by the Church. Blessed Don Bosco was canonized by Pope Pius XI on 1 April 1934.

Chapter 9

St. Elizabeth Ann Seton
1774-1821

Brief Biography

Elizabeth Ann Bayley was born in 1774, and she grew up among the elite of New York high society. Her mother, however, died when she was only three and her stepmother was indifferent toward her. As she grew older, Elizabeth developed a lifelong love for the scriptures. In 1794 she married the wealthy William Seton, but shortly thereafter her husband's business failed and, concurrently, he contracted tuberculosis. In an attempt to save William's life, they went to Italy where William had business friends, but shortly after they arrived he passed away. William's Catholic friends, the Filicchis, were very kind to and supportive of Elizabeth and they, in turn, were impressed by her beautiful soul. Local Italians said that if she were not a Protestant she would be a saint. Elizabeth became interested in Catholicism and the Filicchis gave her instruction in the faith. The brothers never abandoned her and, after she returned to New York, they provided her with a regular stipend of money so that she could look after her family. When Elizabeth's friends found out that she was thinking of becoming a Catholic, they tried to dissuade her, but her desire for the Eucharist and the comfort that she felt knowing that the Blessed Virgin was truly her mother had a great influence on her.

In 1805, after much anguish, she finally entered the Catholic Church. After her first Holy Communion, she wrote: "At last God is mine, and I am His." The president of St. Mary's College suggested that she come to Baltimore to start a school, and Elizabeth accepted the offer. Soon after, two other women joined her in her work and after a wealthy benefactor donated $10,000.00 to them, they moved to Emmitsburg, Maryland, where they established the first free Catholic school in the United States. The women decided to form a sisterhood, and when they adopted a rule they made provision for Elizabeth to keep looking after her children. In March of 1809, she pronounced her vows before Archbishop Carroll of Baltimore, and from that point on she was known as Mother Seton. She still had to endure much hardship and one of her daughters died of tuberculosis at age sixteen. The religious order began to grow, and by 1818 the sisters had established two orphanages and a second school. Elizabeth was full of the kindness of a mother toward her spiritual daughters and students, and they, in turn, loved her. Elizabeth Ann Seton passed away at age forty-six in 1821. Today, six groups of sisters trace their origin to Mother Seton's initial foundation. Elizabeth Ann Seton was beatified by Pope John XXIII in 1963 and was canonized by Pope Paul VI in 1975. Her feast day is January 4. St. Elizabeth Ann Seton's final resting place is the National Shrine of St. Elizabeth Ann Seton located in Emmitsburg, Maryland.

Inspirational Words of Wisdom

- I will go peacefully and firmly to the Catholic Church, for if faith is so important for our salvation, I will seek it where true faith first began, seek it among those who received it from God Himself.

- At last God is mine and I am His—I have received Him.
- The gates of heaven are very low. Only the humble may enter in.
- Cover yourself in prayers and communion with His Precious Blood as the little birds when they see the rising storm, they dip into the ocean.
- My Lord Jesus Christ who was born for me in a stable and died for me upon a cross, say for me in the hour of my death "Father Forgive" and to Thy Mother "Behold your child." Say to me thyself, "This day you will be with me in paradise."
- You can never be bound to speak on any occasion, or on any subject, unless you are sure of doing good by speaking.
- Never let impious customs or the shame of being laughed at, or even the contempt of unreasonable minds, tempt you to treat anyone with the least slight.
- The more we are united to God in love, the nearer we are to those who belong to Him.
- We must often draw the comparison between time and eternity. This is the remedy for all our troubles. How small will the present moment appear when we enter that great ocean.
- Fear nothing so much as not to love enough.
- Now I think for every spark of desire I have ever had to love our God and to show I love, I have now a towering flame.
- The thought of going home, called out by His will—what a transport.

Confirmed Miracles

For Beatification and Canonization

Three miraculous cures attributed to the intercession of Elizabeth Ann Seton were accepted in support of her beatification and canonization. The first of these cures involved Daughter of Charity Sister Gertrude Korzendorfer who, in 1934, was diagnosed by several doctors to have inoperable pancreatic cancer. The sisters in her congregation, along with those who staffed the hospital, began praying to Elizabeth Ann Seton for Sister Gertrude's healing. Miraculously, Sister Gertrude experienced a complete recovery. Subsequently, she went on to resume her duties as the head of a sanitarium in New Orleans.

The second of the three cures attributed to the intercession of Mother Seton was of Anne Theresa O'Neill who, in 1947 at the age of four, was diagnosed with generally fatal acute lymphocytic leukemia. During Holy Week, her breathing had become labored, she could no longer eat, and by all signs the end was near. A relic cloth touched to Mother Seton's remains was pinned to the child's gown. A novena was started, and during the novena Anne Theresa seemed to demonstrate signs of improvement. She began to sit up and eat, and within a few days she was allowed up and walking. Anne continued to improve and, on 27 April 1952, she was discharged from the hospital. Anne's cure was considered acceptable by the Sacred Congregation of Rights in 1959.

The third miracle accepted for Mother Seton's canonization involved Carl Kalin, a sixty-one-year-old construction engineer who fell ill with a rare brain disease called Primary Rubeola Meningoencephalitis. Doctors at the Daughters of Charity's St. Joseph's hospital mentioned that there were only five cases of that kind of disease in the medical books, and all died quickly. Mr. Kalin was already in a coma when the sisters serving in the hospital began to pray to Mother Seton for his recovery. After the fifth day, a relic of Mother Seton was placed on Mr. Kalin's body, and after a few hours he woke up. Five days later he was discharged. On the way out he got on an elevator, and one of the doctors there looked at him and said that he was supposed to be dead. He went back to work and later retired to Florida.

CHAPTER 10

ST. ANDRÉ BESSETTE CSC
1845-1937

Brief Biography

André Bessette was born in 1845 in a small town near Montreal. His father died when he was nine years old, and he lost his mother a few years later. He had poor health throughout his life and no one would have predicted that he would live to ninety-one. He was very pious as a child, and before his father died he encouraged André to develop a devotion to St. Joseph. André never had the opportunity to go to school and so he worked at a number of unskilled jobs in Canada and the United States before he applied for acceptance into the Congregation of the Holy Cross in Montreal. Due to his lack of education, he was admitted as a brother and for forty years did all the menial work for his community.

Subsequently, he served as a doorman at Holy Cross College, where thousands of the poor and despondent began to visit him, seeking his counsel and his prayers. He would tell them the earth is a temporary stopping place; heaven is our real home. Brother André often meditated on the Passion of Jesus, and he would also spend long hours in prayer. Soon he began to manifest the power to heal the sick and, when news of this spread, large numbers of ailing people started coming to the college to see him. The parents of the students at the college began to complain and, consequently, Brother André was given permission to build a chapel on Mount Royal so that the sick could visit him there. Eventually this small chapel became Saint Joseph's Oratory, the largest church dedicated to St. Joseph in the world. Pilgrims came by the thousands, and the healings, which Brother André always attributed to the intercession of St. Joseph, continued unabated. People left their crutches and braces behind in the shrine and others put up plaques to thank St. Joseph. It has been estimated that over his lifetime, Brother André was involved in the healing of 10,000 sick people. Brother André died in January 1937 and, in spite of the winter weather, an estimated one million people from Montreal and the Northeastern United States came to pay their respects to the "Miracle Man of the Mountain." The diocesan process for his beatification was opened within three years of his passing, and Pope John Paul II beatified him on 23 May 1982. He was canonized by Pope Benedict XVI on 17 October 2010, when he became the first saint of the Congregation of the Holy Cross. His feast day is January 6. The body of St. André Bessette is entombed in Saint Joseph's Oratory in Montreal.

Inspirational Words of Wisdom

- You mustn't be sad. It is good to laugh a little.[a]
- It would do healthy men good to visit the sick. This would provide them with good subjects for meditation.[a1]
- The earth is a temporary stopping place. Heaven is our real home.[b]
- If you ate only one meal a week would you survive? It is the same with your soul. Nourish it with the Blessed Sacrament.[c]

- God chose the most ignorant one. If there were anyone more ignorant than I am, then good God would have chosen him.[b]
- People who suffer have something to offer to God. When they succeed in enduring their suffering that is a daily miracle.[d]
- Do not seek to have these trials lifted from you. Instead, ask for the grace to bear them well.[e]
- It is with the smallest brushes that the artist paints the most exquisitely beautiful pictures.[f]
- There is so little distance between heaven and earth that God always hears us. Nothing but a thin veil separates us from God.[g]
- Put yourself in God's hands. He abandons no one.[h]
- If you consider all the saints, you will see that all of them had a devotion to the Blessed Virgin. Her intercession is most powerful; she is the Mother of God and the Mother of men.[i]
- I am nothing. Only a tool in the hands of providence, a lowly instrument at the service of St. Joseph.[j]

Confirmed Miracles

For Beatification

In 1958, Joe Audino had an advanced form of reticulum cell sarcoma throughout his body. His diagnosis was "terminal," and he was expected to die within thirty days. In his troubles he prayed for Br. André's help. He consented to an experimental treatment that never helped anyone else. But shortly after, he was cancer free. His doctor Philip Rubin, of the University of Rochester Cancer Center, said, "There is no clear scientific explanation for his cure." Rubin also wrote in the *Journal of Nuclear Medicine* with a second doctor who was involved that the treatment given Audino "is essentially of no use in the treatment of reticulum cell sarcoma and can lead to death. Remission at this stage of the disease (other than that seen in the case of Mr. Audino) is unknown." Dr. Rubin was so struck by this patient's inexplicable return to health, he was willing to testify to a miracle.

For Canonization

It appears that some of the details of this miracle have been kept confidential. It is known, however, that the stunning recovery of a child who was involved in a traumatic street accident was submitted to the diocesan tribunal in February 2005, the year when Saint Joseph's Oratory of Mount Royal celebrated its 100th anniversary. Unanimously, the doctors, the theologians, and then the Holy Father agreed that it was a scientifically unexplainable healing and was attributed to Blessed Brother André, because the child's parents as well as friends of the family had addressed their prayers to him.

CHAPTER 11

BLESSED DINA BELANGER
(MARIE ST. CECILE DE ROME)
1897-1929

Brief Biography

Dina was born 30 August 1897, in Quebec City, Canada. Beginning at the age of reason, she felt a deep longing for heaven and, as she grew older, she often had mystical experiences and she frequently heard, interiorly, the voice of Jesus speaking with her. When she was sixteen, she asked her spiritual director for permission to enter religious life, but he counseled her to wait until she was in her twenties. She became an accomplished pianist, and at the age of eighteen she traveled to New York to study for two years at the conservatory of music. Subsequently, she gave a number of highly acclaimed concerts throughout Quebec. When she turned twenty-three, she again thought about entering religious life and she felt that Jesus was asking her to join the Congregation of Jesus and Mary. In 1922, Dina took the habit under the name of Mary St. Cecile of Rome, and on 15 August 1923 she made her religious profession.

She was next sent to teach music at one of the Order's convents in Quebec, but this was often interrupted by illness, which was eventually diagnosed to be tuberculosis. As was the case with St. Thérèse of Lisieux, Dina's superior asked her to write an account of her life, which Dina agreed to under obedience, although she regarded it as the most heroic act of

49

her existence. In 1928, Dina made her perpetual vows after which she entered the isolation ward of the infirmary where she remained until September 1929 when, without any struggle and with a radiant smile on her face, God called her home. After her autobiography was published, letters began pouring into her convent from all over the world as many favors were being granted through her intercession. Beginning in 1939, the Archdiocese of Quebec City began its investigation of Dina's life and virtues, and in 1961 her cause was sent to Rome. On 20 March 1993, Dina Belanger, Mother Marie St. Cecile de Rome was beatified by Pope John Paul II. Her tomb is in the convent's chapel.

Inspirational Words of Wisdom

- The heart of Jesus is an abyss of tenderness; that is all I can say because I have no words to express what I now understand.[a]

- Oh if the world could have any suspicion of the delights of paradise, it would not do violence to itself by vainly seeking consolation anywhere else than in genuine goodness.[b]

- Religious life is an uninterrupted exchange between the soul and her bridegroom.[b]

- The heart of the Immaculate Virgin is an abyss of wonders. Enter this most pure sanctuary with respect, and contemplate a masterpiece of purity, love and of every virtue. Mary is a mother. Her great desire is to clothe her children with her own virtues for the glory of Jesus. Learn from her. Ask her to embellish your soul according to the divine ideal. And in the Heart of Mary you will soon come to know the Heart of Jesus.[c]

- Holy Communion for a soul consumed in Jesus is the outpouring of the infinite, the pleasure of sovereign perfection in supreme beauty, the gift of the eternal to the uncreated, the embrace of God the Father and His Word that engenders the Spirit of Love, an outpouring of Love between the three adorable persons, an effusion of tenderness from the heart of indivisible unity.[c]

- Infinite mercy is exercised on our behalf to the extent that it finds us unworthy.[d]

- If the angels could desire anything, it seems to me they would envy us our privilege of suffering as well as the priceless gift of the Eucharist.[e]

- He explained how I could always recognize the difference between His divine voice and that of the tempter. The Savior makes Himself heard only in hours of deep recollection, peace and silence. His voice is so soft that in the soul all must be hushed, while that of the devil is noisy, abrupt and discordant and his words are uttered in the midst of agitation and tumult.[f]

- People in the world often think that our lawful affections grow cold within convent walls. No, it is there that they attain their full maturity. It is there that friendship, freed by grace from all self-seeking, blossoms out into the real flower of charity.[g]

- I felt that Our Lord was granting me a great favor: the Stigmata of His Sacred Wounds. From His Divine Heart, flames radiated on the feet, hands and heart of my annihilated being. He was granting me one of my most cherished desires, but He astonished me by granting it at this moment when I was not expecting it.[h]

- My duty now and my task in eternity is and will be through the Most Blessed Virgin to send forth rays from the heart of Jesus on all souls.[i]
- Blessed be that moment when I will commence in heaven my canticle of thanksgiving.[j]

Confirmed Miracles

For Beatification

In 1939, an infant named Jules Chiasson, of New Brunswick, Canada, was found to have hydrocephalus (water on the brain). He was miraculously cured after his family made a novena to Venerable Dina Belanger.

CHAPTER 12

ST. DAMIEN DE VEUSTER
(APOSTLE TO THE LEPERS)
1840-1889

Brief Biography

Joseph de Veuster was born in 1840 on a farm near Louvain in Belgium. His parents were devout Catholics and raised their eight children accordingly. When Joseph was sixteen, he experienced a call to the priesthood and, consequently, at age eighteen he entered the Congregation of the Sacred Hearts of Jesus and Mary and took the name Damien. At age twenty-three he went as a missionary to Hawaii and, soon after his arrival, he was ordained a priest in Honolulu. Damien was always resourceful: supporting himself by farming, raising livestock, and keeping bees. During the seven years in his parish, he made numerous converts and built many churches and schools, although he had to deal with drunkenness and promiscuity among his parishioners. He once wrote to his parents that there was nothing like an erupting volcano to give you a good idea of hell.

About this time, leprosy began to spread in Hawaii, and to prevent this the government exiled all leprosy patients to the small island of Molokai. There were no doctors, and these sick people were expected to build their own shelters. The lepers wrote to the bishop and asked for a priest, and Damien volunteered his services. There were over 800 lepers on Molokai at that time, and they spent their days playing cards, drinking alcohol, and taking part in prostitution. Damien wrote to his provincial and soon donations were arriving from all over Hawaii. He began by visiting the bedridden, hearing confessions, administering the sacrament of healing, and washing and bandaging the leper's sores. At first he found the sight and especially the smell of the leper's decaying flesh hard to endure, but eventually he got accustomed to it. Damien also established a cemetery, built coffins, and dug proper graves. As soon as he was able to obtain some wood, he also built small houses for the lepers who then started to plant vegetable gardens. Eventually Damien had to enlarge the church to accommodate his many converts, some of whom sang in his church choir.

When he was about forty-five years old, Damien himself contracted leprosy and, realizing that he would soon die, he became concerned about who would care for the children in his two orphanages. Eventually the Franciscan Sister (now saint) Marianne Cope came to Molokai to help Fr. Damien. In addition, a former Trappist named Ira Dutton also arrived and worked tirelessly for the lepers for the next forty-five years. Fr. Damien died a leper for the lepers during Holy Week of 1889. By then he was known and admired throughout the entire world. He was beatified by Pope John Paul II in 1995 and canonized by Pope Benedict XVI in 2009. The state of Hawaii has honored him with a statue which stands in Statuary Hall in the Rotunda of the United States Capitol building in Washington, D.C. Father Damien is buried in St. Anthony's Chapel in Leuven, Belgium. The remains of his right hand were returned to Hawaii and reinterred in his original grave on Molokai.

Inspirational Words of Wisdom

- Turn all your thoughts and aspirations to heaven. Work hard to secure for yourself a place there forever.

- My greatest pleasure is to go to the cemetery to say my beads and to meditate on that unending happiness that so many of them are already enjoying.

- I would not be cured if the cost of the cure was that I must leave the island and give up my work. Do not feel sorry for me.

- My greatest pleasure is in serving the Lord in His poor children rejected by other people.

- The Blessed Sacrament is the stimulus for me to forsake all worldly ambitions.

- After saying Mass, I pick up a saw and with a lot of sweat I have been able to build some chapels that are decent both inside and out. Then a terrible hurricane comes along and knocks them all down.

- Without the constant presence of our Divine Master upon the altars of my poor chapels I never could have preserved casting my lot with the lepers of Molokai.

- They are repugnant to look at, but they also have a soul redeemed at the price of the precious blood of our Divine Savior. He too, in His divine love, consoled lepers.

- Our Lord permits us now and then to pick a beautiful rose from among sharp thorns.

- May the Lord protect me from being carried away by vanity because of certain good which He deigns to permit through my ministry. I am much talked about in the newspapers and in the churches, I wish that all the glory be given to the author and accomplisher of all good. I would desire to remain unknown in the settlement where I am happy and content among my sick children.

- I make myself a leper with the lepers to gain all for Christ. Because of this, when I preach I normally say: "We lepers…"

Confirmed Miracles

For Beatification

In 1895, Sacred Hearts Sister Simplicia Hue was near death in France after suffering seven months from a debilitating intestinal disease. She began a novena to Father Damien and the pain and symptoms of the illness disappeared overnight.

For Canonization

In 1998, a Hawaiian woman named Audrey Toguchi was inflicted with a rare form of cancer which had metastasized to her lungs. Her physician, Dr. Walter Chang, told her: "Nobody has ever survived this cancer. It's going to take you." She prayed at the grave of Father Damien on Molokai and went into remission. She was still alive in 2016.

CHAPTER 13

St. Josephine Bakhita
(Black Mother)
1869-1947

Brief Biography

Josephine Bakhita was born around 1869 in the Darfur region of the Sudan. Her family was loving and very well-off and, although they practiced no particular religious faith, nature itself led Bakhita to sense that there must be some superior being. About this time, a Greek Muslim seized power in Egypt, and he and his army decided to expand his empire into the Sudan where the only wealth they could find to plunder was an abundance of black slaves. When she was about seven, Bakhita was abducted by two slave raiders who eventually sold her to a slave trader, who, in turn, forced her to walk 600 miles to a small city where she was resold to an Arab chief. She was well treated until she committed a small fault, and her master's son beat her unconscious with a whip so that it took a month for her to recover. Bakhita was soon sold to a Turkish general and had to attend to his mother and his wife. For three years she was beaten mercilessly almost every day. Most slaves had to be scarred, and soon it was Bakhita's turn to undergo this torture. She was cut 140 times with a razor and then salt was rubbed into the cuts to ensure maximum scarring. Covered with blood, she was dragged back to her sleeping mat where she lay for over a month unable to move. Bakhita never hated her torturers, and later she prayed for their salvation.

As a result of political unrest, Bakhita's master chose to return to Turkey and, when he reached Khartoum, he sold her to an Italian consular agent who treated her kindly. Subsequently, her Italian master decided to return to Italy, and he took Bakhita with him. While in Genoa he made a gift of Bakhita to a friend and his wife, who took her to Veneto where for the next three years she was a nurse to their daughter. Soon Bakhita was enrolled in the catechumenate in Venice in a boarding school run by the Canossian sisters, and she began to receive instructions in the Christian faith. In due course, Bakhita felt a strong calling to become a Canossian sister herself and was eventually baptized and accepted into the novitiate. Finally on 8 December 1896, she took her vows. For the next five years, Bakhita, also known as Black Mother, remained in Venice, and then she was transferred to the Canossian house in Schio where she remained for the rest of her life. She became the head cook for the community and in 1910, under obedience, she told her life story to another sister who then wrote it down. Later Bakhita became porter and, because she understood what it was to suffer, many would come to see her to draw strength to face life again. Eventually her life story was published and became a best seller. It was soon translated into other languages and tourists started to come to Schio to meet the heroine. As Bakhita grew older, she was confined to a wheelchair and on 8 February 1947, she was called home to God. She was beatified by Pope John Paul II in 1992 and canonized by the same Holy Father in the jubilee year 2000. Her relics are in the Church of the Holy Family of the Canossian convent of Schio.

Inspirational Words of Wisdom

- Seeing the sun, the moon and the stars, I said to myself: Who could be the Master of these beautiful things? And I felt a great desire to see him, to know him and to pay him homage.[a]

- I have given everything to my master: He will take care of me. The best thing for us is not what we consider best but what the Lord wants of us.[b]

- When a person loves another dearly, he desires strongly to be close to the other: therefore, why be afraid to die? The Lord has loved me so much: we must love everyone. We must be compassionate.[c]

- Be good, love the Lord; pray for those who do not know Him. What a great grace it is to know God![c1]

- I travel slowly, one step at a time, because I am carrying two big suitcases. One of them contains my sins, and in the other, which is much heavier, are the infinite merits of Jesus. When I reach heaven I will open the suitcases and say to God: Eternal Father, now you can judge. And to St. Peter: Close the door, because I'm staying.[d]

- He is within me and I am adoring Him.[e]

- If I suffer a bit it does not matter. I owe our Lord so much that what I offer Him is nothing.[e]

- If I were to meet the slave traders who kidnapped me and even those who tortured me, I would kneel and kiss their hands, for if that did not happen, I would not be a Christian and Religious today.[f]

- I am definitely loved and whatever happens to me, I am awaited by this Love. And so my life is good.[g]

Confirmed Miracles

For Beatification

From 1939 onward, a nun from Bakhita's own congregation was bedridden as a result of severe disintegration of her knees, known as arthritic synovitis. In 1948, she prayed a nine-day novena to Bakhita, and one night she awoke with a clear voice saying to her, "Wake up, get up and walk!" The sister obeyed and started walking around the room, something she hadn't done in years. The doctors x-rayed her and found no trace of the disease.

For Canonization

Eva de Costa, a woman from Brazil, was afflicted with diabetic ulcers in her legs. She prayed, "Bakhita, you who suffered so much, please help me, heal my legs!" Her ulcers and pain disappeared at that very moment.

CHAPTER 14

St. Maximillian Kolbe
(Martyr of Auschwitz)
1894-1941

Brief Biography

Raymond Kolbe was born on 8 January 1894, near Lodz, Poland. Once as a young boy, after being scolded by his mother for misbehavior, he asked the Mother of God what was to become of him. He relates what happened next, as follows: "Then she came to me holding two crowns, one white, the other red. She asked if I was willing to accept either of these two crowns. The white one meant that I should persevere in purity, and the red that I should become a martyr. I said that I would accept them both." This vision affected all his future actions. In September 1910, he became a novice in the Franciscan Order and with the habit he took the name Maximillian. From 1912 to 1919 he studied in Rome, where in April 1918 he was ordained a priest. In October 1917, he founded the Crusade of Mary Immaculate (Militia Immaculatae) with the intent of converting sinners, particularly Freemasons, and to bring all to love Our Lady. He returned to Poland and began to publish a monthly review called the Knight of the Immaculate. Around 1927, a Polish prince gave Maximillian some land west of Warsaw, and he and his confreres began to construct one of the largest Franciscan friaries in the world. When it was complete, Niepokalanow (City of the Immaculate) was a self-supporting small city with over 760 inhabitants.

In 1939, however, Nazi Germany invaded Poland, and Fr. Max soon turned Niepokalanow into a shelter for 3,000 Polish refugees, among whom were 2,000 Jews. On 17 February 1941, Fr. Max was arrested and by May of that year he was in the Auschwitz concentration camp. Because he was a priest he was given extra hard labor, and once he was severely beaten and given fifty lashes. When he lost consciousness, he was thrown in the mud and left for dead. Despite his sufferings, Fr. Max never thought of himself but always shared his meager rations with others and spoke to men of the love of God.

One day in July it appeared that three inmates had escaped and so, in reprisal, ten other inmates had to be sent to the starvation bunker. When the ten had been selected, one was crying that he would never see his family again. So Fr. Max volunteered to take his place, and then the men were marched off to the death cell. Fr. Max tried to comfort the others through prayer and hymn singing. After two weeks, all except Fr. Max had died of hunger and thirst. Becoming impatient, the SS men gave him an injection of carbolic acid as well, as his red crown of martyrdom. Father Kolbe died at the age of forty-seven on 14 August 1941, the eve of the Feast of the Assumption. He had completed his mission. In an abyss of human cruelty, he had successfully brought the love of Christ. A faith that can withstand Auschwitz is a faith that can lead many others to God. After the liberation of Auschwitz, Fr. Max's heroism and holiness became known all over the world. Everywhere there were reports of cures brought about by his intercession. On 17 October 1971, Fr. Kolbe was beatified by Pope Paul VI, and on 10 October 1982, Pope John Paul II celebrated his Mass of canonization.

Inspirational Words of Wisdom

- No one in the world can change truth. What we can do and should do is to seek truth and serve it when we have found it. The real conflict is an inner conflict. There are two irreconcilable enemies in the depth of every human soul: good and evil, sin and love. And what use are the victories on the battlefield if we ourselves are defeated in our innermost personal selves?[a]

- The most deadly poison of our time is indifference. And this happens, although the praise of God should know no limits. Let us strive, therefore, to praise him to the greatest extent of our powers.[b]

- The Cross is the school of love.[c]

- Let us remember that love lives through sacrifice and is nourished by giving...Without sacrifice there is no love.[d]

- If angels could be jealous of men, they would be so for one reason: Holy Communion.[e]

- Courage, my sons. Don't you see that we are leaving on a mission? They pay our fare in the bargain. The thing to do now is to pray well in order to win as many souls as possible. [Said when he was first arrested.][f]

- For a book from which to learn how to grow in the love of God, there is no better book than Jesus Christ crucified.[g]

- Be a Catholic: When you kneel before an altar, do it in such a way that others may be able to recognize that you know before whom you kneel.[h]

- If anyone does not wish to have Mary Immaculate for his Mother, he will not have Christ for his Brother.[i]
- Never be afraid of loving the Blessed Virgin too much. You can never love her more than Jesus did.[j]
- Prayer is powerful beyond limits when we turn to the Immaculata who is Queen even of God's heart.[k]
- My aim is to institute perpetual adoration, for this is the most important activity.[l]
- The soul offers to the Immaculate its own acts of love, not as one consigns an object to just any intermediary, but as her property, as her complete and exclusive property, since it understands that the Immaculate offers to Jesus these acts as if they were her own, which means that she offers them without stain, immaculate; Jesus, then, offers them to the Father.[m]

Confirmed Miracles

Beatification

In 1948, Angela Testoni was suffering from intestinal tuberculosis. She prayed to Maximilian Kolbe to intercede for her, and she was cured of her disease. Similarly, in 1950, Francis Ranier had developed calcification of the arteries. After praying to Maximilian Kolbe, he was also healed.

Canonization

Maximilian Kolbe was canonized by Pope John Paul II who declared that St. Maximilian was to be venerated as a martyr for charity.

CHAPTER 15

ST. FAUSTINA KOWALSKA
(ST. MARIA FAUSTINA KOWALSKA OF THE BLESSED SACRAMENT)
1905-1938

Brief Biography

Helena Kowalska was born in Poland on 25 August 1905, into a poor but religious family. When she was nineteen years old and praying in Lodz Cathedral, as she later recounted, Jesus instructed her to depart for Warsaw immediately and to enter a convent. Without her parents' permission, she went to Warsaw and entered a church to ask the priest for instructions. He arranged for her lodging, and she was finally accepted into the convent of the Sisters of our Lady of Mercy where, on 30 April 1926, she was clothed in the habit and received the religious name of Sister Maria Faustina of the Blessed Sacrament. In April 1928, she completed her novitiate and took her first religious vows as a nun. Later, in 1930, she was transferred to the convent in Plock, Poland. On the night of Sunday, 22 February 1931, she wrote in her diary:

> While I was in my cell Jesus appeared wearing a white garment with red and pale rays emanating from His heart. He instructed me to paint an image according to the pattern you see, with the signature: "Jesus, I trust in you." He said, "I desire that this image be venerated, first in your chapel, and then

throughout the world. I promise that the soul that will venerate this image will not perish."

Jesus also told her that he wanted the Divine Mercy image to be solemnly blessed on the first Sunday after Easter Sunday; that Sunday is to be the Feast of Mercy. Sister Faustina approached several other sisters in the Plock convent about making a portrait of the image Jesus had revealed to her, but none would agree. She was later transferred to their convent in Vilnius (still in Poland) where she met Father Michał Sopoćko who helped her to find an artist who consented to paint the first Divine Mercy image. On 13 September 1935, while still in Vilnius, Sister Faustina wrote in her diary of a vision about the Chaplet of Divine Mercy. The purpose of the chaplet's prayers for mercy are threefold: to obtain mercy, to trust in Christ's mercy, and to show mercy to others. In 1936, Fr. Sopoćko wrote the first brochure on the Divine Mercy devotion, which had the Divine Mercy image on the cover. Later, in 1936, Faustina became ill with what was likely tuberculosis, so she was moved to the sanatorium in Krakow where she continued to spend time reciting the chaplet, praying for the conversion of sinners, and keeping her diary. She went to her reward at the age of thirty-three on 5 October 1938, and now rests in Kraków's Basilica of Divine Mercy. By 1941, the Divine Mercy devotion had reached the United States, and millions of copies of Divine Mercy prayer cards have been printed and distributed worldwide. Sister Faustina was beatified on 18 April 1993, and was canonized by Pope John Paul II on 30 April 2000.

Inspirational Words of Wisdom

- Patience, prayer, and silence—these are what give strength to the soul.[a]

- Pure love—knows that only one thing is needed to please God—to do even the smallest things out of great love.[b]
- Suffering is the greatest treasure on earth—it purifies the soul.[c]
- Love endures everything, love is stronger than death, love fears nothing.[d]
- Oh, if the suffering soul knew how it is loved by God, it would die of joy and excess happiness. Someday, we will know the value of suffering but then we will no longer be able to suffer. The present moment is ours.[c1]
- I know well that the greater and more beautiful the work is, the more terrible will be the storms that rage against it.[e]
- The soul does not benefit from the sacrament of confession if it is not humble. Pride keeps it in darkness.[f]
- We do not know the number of souls that is ours to save through our prayers and sacrifices. Therefore, let us always pray for sinners.[g]
- There are three ways of performing an act of mercy: the merciful word by forgiving and comforting; secondly, prayer, for this too is mercy; and third, deeds of mercy. And when the Last Day comes, we shall be judged from this, and on this basis we shall receive the eternal verdict.[h]
- Every morning during meditation, I prepare myself for the whole day's struggle. Holy Communion assures me that I will win the victory.[c1]

- He who wants to learn true humility should reflect on the Passion of Jesus.ⁱ
- Let no one doubt concerning the goodness of God, even if a person's sins were as dark as night. One thing alone is necessary, that the sinner set ajar the door of his heart, be it ever so little, to let in a ray of God's merciful grace, and then God will do the rest.^j
- From today onwards, I am going to strive for the greatest purity of soul, that the rays of God's grace may be reflected in all their brilliance. ^{c1}
- Great love can change small things into great ones, and it is only love which lends value to our actions.^k
- Jesus, I trust in you.^l

Confirmed Miracles

For Beatification

Maureen Digan had suffered for decades from lymphedema, a disease that causes significant swelling from fluid retention. She had undergone ten operations, including a leg amputation. In March 1981, when Digan was praying at Kowalska's tomb, she heard a voice saying, "Ask for my help and I will help you," and her constant pain ceased. After two days, her foot, which because of swelling had been too large for her shoe, was healed. Upon her return to the United States, five Boston area physicians stated that she was healed, and the case was declared miraculous.

For Canonization

Father Ronald Pytel experienced cardiac failure in his more advanced years. In June 1995, during his recovery from heart surgery, he prayed the Chaplet of Divine Mercy every day, and he celebrated a Mass on 5 October, Faustina's feast day. Starting on the night of the Mass, the priest found that taking his heart medication caused unexpected chest pain that he had not experienced prior to the Mass. He consulted with Dr. Nicholas Fortuin, who found Pytel's heart to be completely normal and healthy. Dr. Valentin Fuster has since confirmed that the total healing of Pytel's heart occurred within three days of the Mass on 5 October 1995.

CHAPTER 16

St. Joseph Moscati
(Doctor of the Poor)
1880-1927

Brief Biography

Joseph Moscati was born 25 July 1880, in Benevito, Italy. His family were devout Catholics who instilled in young Joseph a love for the Eucharist and for Our Lady. He excelled at school and, when he was a young man, he entered Naples University where he earned a first-class honors degree in medicine and surgery. At the age of twenty-two, he began to practice medicine, seeing Christ in each of his patients. He was known to carry a rosary in his pocket to keep Jesus and, in turn, our Blessed Mother close to him whenever he needed to make important decisions. In 1911, he passed the exam for medical coadjutor of the United Hospitals, and in July he was chosen for the university chair in chemical physiology. In addition, he studied and became proficient in twenty other medical specialties so as to best serve others. Thus, he was soon recognized as one of the most outstanding teachers and scientists among his peers, including those who were hostile to religion.

In 1915, Italy declared war against Austria, and Joseph volunteered to minister to both the bodies and the souls of the wounded. When peace was declared, Joseph became head of the Department for Incurables. In the hospital and in his private practice, he was convinced that the first condition for wellness was to be close to God, and so he often recommended that patients who were about to undergo surgery first receive the sacraments. Although the rich and famous often sought his care, the poor, the homeless, and priests and religious were his preferred patients. He accomplished much good, rarely accepted payment for his services and would also frequently pay for his patient's prescriptions. After some rather extraordinary cures, He would counsel: "If you want to pay, go to confession, for it was God who healed you." Eventually, Dr. Moscati's intense schedule began to affect his health. On 12 April 1927, he began his day as usual with Mass and communion. He worked at the hospital and then returned to his home to begin examining the large number of patients waiting for him. In the mid-afternoon he felt ill and retired to his bedroom where, sitting in a chair and without agony or speaking again, he gently passed on to his reward. As soon as the news of his death became known, his body became the site of continuous pilgrimage and people began referring to him as a saint. After his death, many miraculous cures were reported and Dr. Moscati was often seen standing by the sick person when he was healed. Joseph Moscati was beatified in 1975 by Pope Paul VI and canonized in 1987 by Pope John Paul II. His reliquary is in the church of Gesu Nuovo in Naples, Italy.

Inspirational Words of Wisdom

- Love the truth, appear as you are, and without affectation and without fear and without human respect. Even if the truth costs you persecution, accept it; and if it means anguish, endure it. And if for the sake of truth you should have to sacrifice yourself and your life, then be strong in your sacrifice. (St. Joseph Moscati written as a note to himself).

- Remember that in pursuing medicine you have assumed responsibility for a sublime mission. Persevere, with God in your heart, with the teachings of your father and your mother always in your memory, with love and devotion for the abandoned, with faith and enthusiasm, deaf to praises and criticisms, steadfast against envy, and inclined only to do good. (St. Joseph Moscati to a young doctor).

- Blessed are we doctors if we remember that we have in the presence of sick people not only bodies to cure but also divine and eternal souls, and we must love them as ourselves.

- Remember that you must treat not only bodies but also souls with counsel that appeals to their minds and hearts rather than with cold prescriptions.

- Let us practice charity, let us not forget to make an offering of our actions every day, every moment, doing everything for loves sake.

- Life doesn't end with death; it continues in a better way. It has been promised to everyone after the world's redemption, the day that will join us again to our beloved dead and that will bring us again to Supreme Love.

- Charity changed the world. Anyone can be an everlasting symbol of life eternal, where death is nothing but a step, a metamorphosis towards a higher place, if they will dedicate themselves to good.

- I'm just trying. The only thing that can cure you is Jesus. Always pray to Him because He is the source of all healing.

- Beauty and enchantment of life pass away, there remains only eternal love surviving in us, which is our hope for love is God. The grandeur of death is not the end, but the beginning of the Sublime and the Divine, in whose presence flowers and beauty are as nothing.

Confirmed Miracles

For Beatification

In 1923, Costantino Nazzaro fell ill with Addison's disease, for which there was no cure. In 1954, he went to the church of Gesù Nuovo and prayed before the tomb of St. Joseph Moscati, returning there every fifteen days for four months. Subsequently, Mr. Nazarro dreamt of being operated on by St. Joseph Moscati who replaced the atrophied part of his body with live tissues and advised him not to take any more medicines. The next morning, Mr. Nazzaro was healed. The doctors who visited him could not explain the unexpected recovery.

In 1941, Raffaele Perrotta was diagnosed with meningococcal cerebrospinal meningitis. Shortly afterwards, Raffaele's condition worsened so much that the little boy's mother asked for the intervention of St. Joseph Moscati, leaving the image of the doctor of the poor under her baby's pillow. A few hours after the desperate gesture of the mother, the child was perfectly healed. His doctors reported: "There are two incontrovertible data: the severity of the syndrome and the immediate and complete resolution of the disease."

For Canonization

In 1978, twenty-nine-year-old Giuseppe Montefusco was diagnosed with acute myeloblastic leukemia, a disease that had a single prognosis: death. Giuseppe's mother was desperate, but one night she dreamt of a doctor wearing a white coat. Comforted by this, the woman talked about it with her priest who identified the doctor as Joseph Moscati. The whole family began to pray every day that the doctor of the poor would intercede for a miraculous healing for Giuseppe Montefusco, and less than a month later their prayers were answered.

CHAPTER 17

St. Katharine Drexel
1858-1955

Brief Biography

Katharine Drexel was born in Philadelphia on 26 November 1858. A mere month after Katharine's birth, her mother died. Two years later her father married a devout Catholic who raised Katharine and her two sisters in the faith, teaching them responsible charity to the poor. The family attended Mass together every morning and, being enormously wealthy, they also travelled extensively. In 1879, Katharine's stepmother was stricken with cancer, and Katharine nursed her for three years until she died. Two years hence, Katharine's father also passed away, leaving almost all of his multimillion-dollar fortune to his three daughters. Almost immediately, the three sisters began supporting a number of charitable works, including the Catholic Native American missions. In 1887, the sisters visited the missions in the Dakotas, and Katharine was very disturbed by the poverty she saw there, so she arranged to fund them from her own fortune. Within four years, the sisters built thirteen mission schools in several western states, and within twenty years they would contribute more than a million and a half dollars toward Catholic education.

Although both of her sisters married, Katharine felt more and more called to the religious life. After consulting with her spiritual director, it was decided that she should start a new religious order that would work for the salvation of the African American and First Nations people. In 1889, Katharine entered the novitiate of the Sisters of Mercy, and in 1891 she professed her vows as the first Sister of the Blessed Sacrament. Immediately after, Sister Katharine opened a novitiate for her new order and by the end of the year there were twenty-one members in the community. They began in Philadelphia by establishing a boarding school for poor children, and eventually their spiritual director allowed a group of sisters to open a second boarding school at the mission in Santa Fe, New Mexico. Sister Katharine's two blood sisters also continued to support her order's work and throughout the South they established a system of Catholic schools for African American children. By 1942, their foundations included thirty convents, forty mission centers, and twenty-three rural schools. In 1915, Mother Katharine established Xavier University in New Orleans, the first United States institution of higher learning for African Americans. In 1935, Mother Katharine suffered a severe heart attack and had to retire to an infirmary where for the next twenty years she spent her days in prayer. On 3 March 1955, Mother Katharine peacefully slipped away; at that time there were more than 600 Sisters of the Blessed Sacrament. Katharine Drexel was beatified in 1988 by Pope John Paul II and canonized in 2000 by the same Holy Father. Her resting place is located in the Katharine Drexel Shrine in the Cathedral of St. Peter and St. Paul in Philadelphia.

Inspirational Words of Wisdom

- If we wish to serve God and love our neighbor well, we must manifest our joy in the service we render to Him and them. Let us open wide our hearts. It is joy that invites us. Press forward and fear nothing.[a]
- It is a lesson we all need—to let alone the things that do not concern us. He has other ways for oth-

ers to follow Him; all do not go by the same path. It is for each of us to learn the path by which He requires us to follow Him, and to follow Him on that path.[b]

- Ours is the spirit of the Eucharist, the total gift of self.[c]

- My sweetest joy is to be in the presence of Jesus in the Holy Sacrament. I beg that when obliged to withdraw in body, I may leave my heart before the Holy Sacrament.[d]

- The patient and humble endurance of the cross, whatever nature it may be, is the highest work we have to do.[e]

- Holiness consists of one thing: to do God's will, as He wills it, because He wills it.[f]

- The passive way—I abandon myself to it, not in a multiplicity of trials, extraordinary penances, practices of great works—but in peaceful abandonment to the tenderness of Jesus, which I must try to imitate, and by being in constant union with His meek and humble heart.[h]

- Lord, help me to love you in the way you deserve to be loved.[i]

- If we are disciples of Jesus, we shall be happy to spend ourselves and be spent for the salvation of souls.[j]

- Teach me to know your Son intimately, to love Him ardently and to follow Him closely.[k]

Confirmed Miracles

For Beatification

In 1974, young Robert Gutherman was admitted to St. Cristopher's Hospital for surgery on his right ear. The doctors discovered that Robert had only one of the three small bones usually found in the ear canal, and he also had a perforated ear drum. It was determined he would never be able to hear again. Meanwhile, the Sisters of the Blessed Sacrament had been praying daily with Robert and his mother. After dismissal from the hospital, Robert went for a checkup and the doctor realized that he had a perfect ear drum and normal hearing. In 1988, Robert Gutherman's healing was accepted as the first miracle of Saint Katharine Drexel.

For Canonization

In September 1993, Amy Wall's hearing threshold was 90 decibels, meaning she could barely hear shouting. In November 1993, Amy's mother obtained a second-class relic of Blessed Katharine from the Sisters of the Blessed Sacrament. She pressed it to Amy's ear, and the Wall family began praying to Katharine Drexel for a miracle. In March 1994, a preschool teacher at the school for the deaf saw dramatic changes in Amy's response to sound and subsequent tests showed that she could hear normally in both ears. In 2000, Amy Wall's healing was accepted as the second miracle of Saint Katharine Drexel.

CHAPTER 18

BL. JERZY POPIELUSZKO
(VICTIM OF THE COMMUNISTS)
1947-1984

Brief Biography

Jerzy Popieluszko was born in 1947 into a poor farm family in Eastern Poland. As a young boy, he would walk three miles every morning before school to serve Mass at the closest church. St. Maximilian Kolbe was one of his heroes, and after high school Jerzy enrolled in a seminary in Warsaw to be near to St. Max's former friary. After his first year in seminary, Jerzy was conscripted into an army indoctrination unit where, because of his faith, he was given extra-hard labor, severely beaten, and put into isolation for a month. All of this ruined his health, although he told a seminary master: "One does not suffer when one suffers for Christ." Jerzy was ordained in 1972 and assigned to St. Stanislaw Kostka Church near the Warsaw steel mill. In 1980 the workers had won the right to collectivization and so they established the Solidarity Trade Union. They wanted to celebrate Mass and the frail Fr. Jerzy answered their call, impressing the workers with his straight talk about overcoming evil with good. Subsequently, Jerzy made a vow to stay with these men as long as he could, and he soon became the spiritual patron of the Solidarity movement. When the Union was forced underground and martial law was imposed, he used his rectory as a center to look after both the temporal and spiritual needs of his parishioners.

In spite of martial law, Father Jerzy began to celebrate a monthly Mass for the Fatherland, and Poles from all over the country came to attend these liturgies. The Warsaw bureau chief for the New York Times wrote that: "Nowhere else in the Soviet Empire could anyone stand before a crowd of 15,000 people and tell them that defiance of the Communist authorities was an obligation of the heart, of religion, of manhood, and of nationhood." The Times bureau chief was not the only one who noticed, so did the Polish secret police. So they decided to kill Fr. Jerzy Popieluszko. He began to receive death threats, and one evening a bomb exploded in his rectory, which would have killed him had he been in the same room. On 19 October 1984, Fr. Jerzy's car was stopped by the secret police, and he was beaten with fists and clubs. He was then bound and gagged and subsequently drowned in a water reservoir. On the day of Fr. Jerzy's funeral, half a million people filled the streets leading up to St. Stanislaw's church, as once again the country stood united around its heroic martyr priest. Fr. Jerzy Popieluszko was beatified a martyr on 6 June 2010, by Archbishop Angelo Amato on behalf of Pope Benedict XVI. A miracle attributed to his intercession and required for his canonization is now under investigation. His tomb is in St. Stanislaw Kostka Church.

Inspirational Words of Wisdom:

- It is not enough for a Christian to condemn evil, cowardice, lies, and use of force, hatred, and oppression. He must at all times be a witness to and defender of justice, goodness, truth, freedom, and love. He must never tire of claiming these values as a right both for himself and others.[a]

- Truth like justice is connected to love. And love has a price.[b]
- One does not suffer when one suffers for Christ.[c]
- True love is demanding; it requires sacrifice. Truth too must cost something. Truth that does not cost anything is a lie.[d]
- Truth never changes, it cannot be destroyed by any decision or legal act. Telling the truth with courage is a way leading directly to freedom. A man who tells the truth is a free man despite external imprisonment.[e]
- An idea that needs rifles to survive dies of its own accord.[a1]
- Let us pray to God to set us free from fear and terror but, first and foremost, free from the desire for violence and vengeance.[f]
- Justice and the right to know the truth require of us from this pulpit to repeatedly demand a limit on the tyranny of censorship.[g]
- Be with them Holy Mother. Be with them, to those condemned to forced isolation without a trial, with all those who suffer from the imprisonment of their loved ones. When it was suggested to our Polish brothers to leave the country, you were saying with pain in your voice, it is impossible that there is no place for Poles in Poland. Everyone has the right to live in their homeland. No one should be condemned to exile.[h]

Confirmed Miracles:

For Beatification

Jerzy Popieluszko was beatified a martyr. Hence, no miracle was required.

CHAPTER 19

St. Frances Cabrini
1850-1917

Brief Biography

Maria Francesca Cabrini was born on 15 July 1850, into a farm family in a region of Italy that was then part of the Austrian Empire. She was small and weak as a child and remained in delicate health throughout her life. At thirteen, Francesca enrolled in a school run by the Daughters of the Sacred Heart of Jesus, and five years later she graduated cum laude, with a teaching certificate. In 1870, she applied for admission to the Daughters of the Sacred Heart, but they told her, reluctantly, that she was too frail to endure their rigorous life. Consequently, she became a teacher and later headmistress at the House of Providence orphanage in Codogno, where she also helped to establish a small community of women devoted to living the religious life.

In November 1880, she and seven of her now grown orphan girls founded the Missionary Sisters of the Sacred Heart of Jesus (M.S.C.), and Francesca added Xavier to her name to honor Saint Francis Xavier, the patron of missionary service. They took in orphans and foundlings and established seven homes and a free school in their first five years. These good works brought Frances Cabrini to the attention of Pope Leo XIII, who asked her to go to the United States to help Italian immigrants who were living in great poverty.

She left for the United States on 31 March 1889, along with six other sisters. On arrival in New York, they established the Sacred Heart Orphan Asylum to provide for the needs of the many orphans, and organized catechism and education classes for the Italian immigrants. Frances was as resourceful as she was prayerful, finding people who would donate what she needed in money and other support. In New York City, she also founded Columbus Hospital, which merged with the Italian Hospital to become Cabrini Medical Center. Soon, requests for her assistance started to come from all over the world. She traveled throughout the United States as well as to Europe and Central and South America making twenty-three trans-Atlantic crossings and establishing sixty-seven institutions, including schools, hospitals, and orphanages.

In 1909, Frances Cabrini became a naturalized United States citizen. However, a few years later, she died of complications from malaria in her own Columbus Hospital in Chicago. She was beatified on 13 November 1938, by Pope Pius XI, and canonized on 7 July 1946, by Pope Pius XII. In 1933, her body was exhumed and divided as part of the process toward sainthood. At that time, her head was removed and is preserved in the chapel of the congregation's international motherhouse in Rome. Her heart is preserved in Codogno, where she founded her missionary order, an arm bone is in her national shrine in Chicago, and most of the rest of her body is enshrined in the chapel of St. Mother Cabrini High School in New York City.

Inspirational Words of Wisdom:

- I will go anywhere and do anything in order to communicate the love of Jesus to those who do not know Him or have forgotten Him.

- If you are in danger, if your hearts are confused, turn to Mary; she is our comfort, our help; turn towards her and you will be saved.
- We must pray without tiring, for the salvation of mankind does not depend on material success but on Jesus alone.
- Prayer is powerful! It fills the earth with mercy. Along the course of the centuries wonderful works have been achieved through prayer.
- Those who pray with faith have fervor, and fervor is the fire of prayer. This mysterious fire has the power of consuming all our faults and imperfections and of giving to our actions vitality, beauty, and merit.
- The world is poisoned with erroneous theories, and needs to be taught sane doctrines, but it is difficult to straighten what has become crooked.
- The impressions of childhood are never lost.
- Speak often of heaven to those who approach you, make them love it as well as the virtues which are required before we can be admitted to our beloved country. For if you know how to draw souls there by your zeal, your good example, and your exemplary religious conduct, you may be assured the gates will be opened for you also.
- Go often my dear ones and place yourself at the feet of Jesus. He is our comfort, our way, and our life.
- The science of suffering is the science of the saints. Let us then be glad when an unexpected cross presents itself, and we are afflicted with pain.
- Mary is the mysterious book of predestination to glory.

- Did a Magdalene, a Paul, a Constantine or an Augustine become mountains of ice after their conversion? Quite the contrary. We should never have had these prodigies of conversion and marvelous holiness if they had not changed the flames of human passion into volcanoes of immense love of God.

- This world is so small. To me, space is as an imperceptible object, as I am accustomed to dwell in eternity.

Confirmed Miracles

For Beatification

Peter Smith was born 14 March 1921, in Manhattan's Columbus Hospital which was staffed by Mother Cabrini's Missionary Sisters of the Sacred Heart of Jesus. A nurse mistakenly put a 50% solution, rather than a 1% solution, of silver nitrate into the newborn's eyes to protect them from bacterial infections. Peter was evaluated by an eye specialist who said flatly: "The corneas are gone. Nobody can do anything." The Superior of the hospital touched a relic of Mother Cabrini to little Peter's eyes, then pinned the relic to his nightgown and, with her sisters, spent the entire night praying in the hospital's chapel. When the doctors inspected the baby's eyes again, they found the corneas were intact and the eyes were perfectly normal. Peter's eyesight had been restored! The joy of the moment was short-lived, however, when that same day little Peter got double pneumonia and his temperature reached 108 degrees Fahrenheit. The superior told his doctor: "Mother Cabrini has not cured his eyes just to let him die of pneumonia." The sisters prayed yet again for a miracle, and by the next morning all traces of the pneumonia in the boy had disappeared.

The second miracle involved Sister Delfina of the Missionary Sisters of the Sacred Heart of Jesus. In 1914 she immigrated to the United States, and in 1916 went west to Seattle. By 1925 Sister Delfina could no longer hold anything in her stomach, and after four major operations she refused any further treatment. She could not even stand up; she was so weak. Her bishop suggested that she pray to Mother Cabrini, and she complied along with all of her co-religious. Finally, on the night of 14 December 1925, she saw Mother Cabrini who told her: "I'm going to send you to work." Then she smiled and disappeared. The next day, Sister Delfina ate three meals and kept them all down. She lived for forty-two more years following her cure, dying at the age of seventy-six.

For Canonization

The two additional miracles needed for canonization both occurred in Lombard, Italy, near where Mother Cabrini was born. The first involved Paulo Pezini, who, while still a youth, was kicked in the stomach by a horse. This led to chronic severe pain and hemorrhaging. In early 1939, he also came down with double pneumonia with chills, fever and sepsis, followed by cardiac arrest, kidney failure, and coma. His friends and doctor began a novena to Bl. Frances Cabrini, asking for a cure. The patient suddenly woke up, and his doctors confirmed he was in perfect health. All his medical problems had miraculously disappeared.

The final miracle concerned Ettore Paggetti, a locomotive engineer who was badly burned in an accident. Medical assistance was deemed futile so prayers were offered for the intercession of Mother Cabrini. The prayers were answered and Mr. Paggetti was completely healed.

CHAPTER 20

St. Óscar Romero
(Martyr of the Americas)
1917-1980

Brief Biography

Óscar Romero was born on 15 August 1917, into a very poor family in the mountains of El Salvador. At the age of thirteen, he entered the minor seminary in San Miguel and progressed all the way to the Gregorian University in Rome where he earned the licentiate in theology. He was ordained a priest in Rome in 1942 and celebrated his first Mass in his home village in January 1944. He was appointed parish priest in San Miguel where he served for the next thirty years. In 1970, Fr. Romero was ordained auxiliary bishop of San Salvador and was subsequently appointed bishop of his home diocese where he saw the extent of grinding rural poverty: children dying from preventable diseases and denied opportunity for education to ensure they would have to remain field laborers, people paid less than half the minimum wage, and others beaten viciously for daring to ask for long overdue salaries. When five peasants were killed by national guardsmen, Romero personally protested to their commander who replied with death threats.

In early 1977, Romero became archbishop of San Salvador, and he began by listening to his priests and lay people, incorporating their concerns into his homilies. He also attempted to get state authorities to investigate the murders in his diocese by sending strong letters to the president of the country. Romero distanced himself, however, from Marxist ideology and called constantly for reconciliation and not class warfare. Nevertheless, priests were arrested and exiled and churches were desecrated, and it became evident that the violence against the poor was linked to a deep hatred for the Catholic Church.

One of the last things Archbishop Romero did was to send a letter to President Carter asking him to stop shipping arms to the government of El Salvador, as these were being used to kill his people. In his second to last Sunday homily, he spoke to the death squads: "Let them stop killing those of us who are trying to achieve a more just society. I speak in the first person because I received notice that I am to be eliminated next week." In his final Sunday homily on 23 March 1980, he appealed to the enlisted men in the National Guard and the police, reminding them that no soldier is required to obey an order that is against the law of God. He continued: "I beg you, I beseech you, I order you in the name of God. Stop the repression." The next day Archbishop Romero was shot dead by a lone assassin while he was offering the Holy Mass. It is estimated that 200,000 people attended his funeral Mass including a large number of priests and bishops from all over the world. Óscar Romero was beatified a martyr by Pope Francis on 23 May 2015, and canonized a saint on 14 October 2018, by the same Holy Father. His tomb is in the cathedral in San Salvador.

Inspirational Words of Wisdom

- There are many things that can only be seen through eyes that have cried.[a]

- The ones who have a voice must speak for those who are voiceless.[b]
- We cannot do everything, and there is a sense of liberation in realizing that. This enables us to do something, and to do it very well. It may be incomplete, but it is a beginning, a step along the way, an opportunity for the Lord's grace to enter and do the rest.[c]
- Aspire not to have more, but to be more.[d]
- Peace is the product of justice and love.[e]
- Let us not tire of preaching love; it is the force that will overcome the world. Let us not tire of preaching love. Though we see that waves of violence succeed in drowning the fire of Christian love, love must win out; it is the only thing that can.[f]
- We must not seek the child Jesus in the pretty figures of our Christmas cribs. We must seek him among the undernourished children who have gone to bed at night with nothing to eat, among the poor newsboys who will sleep covered with newspapers in doorways.[g]
- Beautiful is the moment in which we understand that we are no more than an instrument of God; we live only as long as God wants us to live; we can only do as much as God makes us able to do; we are only as intelligent as God would have us be.[h]
- You can tell the people that if they succeed in killing me, that I forgive and bless those who do it. Hopefully, they will realize they are wasting their time. A bishop will die, but the church of God, which is the people, will never perish.[i]

- Let us take seriously the cause of the poor as though it were our own.[j]
- Each time we look upon the poor, on the farmworkers who harvest the coffee, the sugarcane, or the cotton...remember, there is the face of Christ.[k]
- Peace is not the product of terror or fear. Peace is not the silence of cemeteries. Peace is not the silent result of violent repression. Peace is the generous, tranquil contribution of all to the good of all. Peace is dynamism. Peace is generosity. It is right, and it is duty.[l]
- That is the hope that inspires Christians. We know that every effort to better society, especially when injustice and sin are so ingrained, is an effort that God blesses, that God wants, that God demands of us.[m]
- When we leave Mass, we ought to go out the way Moses descended Mt. Sinai: with his face shining, with his heart brave and strong to face the world's difficulties.[n]

Confirmed Miracles:

For Beatification

Óscar Romero was beatified a martyr, and, therefore, no miracle was required.

For Canonization

Cecilia Maribel Flores, a Salvadoran woman, after undergoing an emergency cesarean section for her third child, developed an infection that left her in a coma. Suffering from internal hemorrhaging and with her kidneys on the verge of collapse, she was not expected to survive. Her husband began to pray to Óscar Romero to help his wife, and exactly at that time Cecilia Flores began to get better. She proceeded to a complete recovery. Her doctors considered her cure to be miraculous.

CHAPTER 21

St. Gianna Molla
(Saint for the Unborn)
1922-1962

Brief Biography

Gianna Beretta was born on 4 October 1922, into a devoutly religious family in Magenta, Italy. One of her relatives was the Servant of God, Enrico Beretta, and several others were priests and religious sisters. In 1927 the Berettas relocated to Genoa where she attended school and was an active participant in parish life. In 1942 she began her studies in medicine in Milan where she was also a member of the Catholic Action movement. In November 1949, Gianna received her medical diploma, and in 1952 she became a specialist in pediatrics. If any of her patients were poor, like St. Joseph Moscati before her, she would provide a free medical examination as well as medicine and money. In December 1954, she started seeing the engineer Pietro Molla (1912 -2010) and the two were married the following September by Fr. Giuseppe Beretta, Gianna's brother. Following their marriage, Gianna and Pietro had three children: Pierluigi (1956), Mariolina (1957), and Laura (1959). In 1961, during the second month of her fourth and final pregnancy, Gianna developed a fibroma on her uterus. The doctors gave her three choices: an abortion, a complete hysterectomy, or the removal of the fibroma alone. The Church forbade all direct abortion, but teachings on the principle of double effect would have allowed her to undergo the hysterectomy which would have caused her unborn child's death as an unintended consequence.

Gianna opted for the removal of the fibroma as she wanted to preserve her child's life; she told the doctors that her child's life was more important than her own. On the morning of 21 April 1962, Holy Saturday, Gianna was sent to the hospital where her fourth child, Gianna Emanuela, was delivered via a caesarean section. But Gianna continued to have severe pain and died of septic peritonitis one week after giving birth. Her daughter, Gianna Emanuela, still lives and is a doctor of geriatrics. In April 1971, Gianna's husband wrote a biographical account of her life and dedicated it to their children. He often told Gianna Emanuela that her mother's choice was one of conscience as both a loving mother and a doctor. In November 1972, the cardinal archbishop of Milan promoted the opening of a cause for Gianna Molla, and in March 1980 the beatification process was opened under Pope John Paul II. In April 1994, after approval of a miracle in response to Molla's intercession, she was beatified by Pope John Paul II. Following the approval of a second miracle, she was proclaimed a saint of the Church by the same Holy Father in May 2004. Gianna's husband and their children were present at the canonization. It was the first time that a husband had ever witnessed his wife's canonization. St. Gianna Molla is buried next to her husband in a small edifice in a cemetery located near the Sanctuary of St. Gianna Molla in Mesero, Italy.

Inspirational Words of Wisdom

- Love and sacrifice are closely linked, like the sun and the light. We cannot love without suffering and we cannot suffer without love.[a]

- Our body is a monstrance: through its crystal the world should see God.[b]
- One earns Paradise with one's daily task.[c]
- The secret of happiness is to live moment by moment and to thank God for all that He, in His goodness, sends to us day after day.[d]
- In order to bring peace back to my soul, the only way that there exists on the Earth is Confession, because Jesus awaits me with His immense heart.[e]
- As to the past, let us entrust it to God's mercy, the future to divine providence, our task is to live holy the present moment.[f]
- Lord, keep your grace in my heart. Make it that I may bear every day some flowers and some fruit.[g]
- We must be living witnesses of the beauty and the grandeur of Christianity.[h]
- The stillness of prayer is the most essential condition for fruitful action. Before all else the disciple kneels down.[i]
- Love your children. In them you can see baby Jesus. Pray for them a lot and every day put them under Holy Mary's protection.[j]
- The great mystery of man is Jesus. He who visits a sick person helps me Jesus said. We touch Jesus in the bodies of our patients. Our mission is not finished when medicines are no longer of use. We must bring the soul to God; our word has some authority. Catholic doctors are so necessary.[k]

Confirmed Miracles

For Beatification

Lucia Sylvia Cirilo, a protestant Brazilian woman, gave birth to a stillborn child on 22 October 1977. Her doctors found an unseen complication that caused a rectovaginal fistula which the hospital was not equipped to handle. She was told that she had to be moved to the hospital at São Luís, but she knew that she would not survive the relocation. One of the nurses, Sister Bernardina de Manaus, appealed for the intercession of Gianna Molla while looking at a small picture of her. The sister asked two other nurses to follow her lead and the group soon discovered that Cirilo's pain had disappeared with the doctors amazed at the fact that the fistula had healed in full.

For Canonization

Elizabeth Comparini, another Brazilian woman, was sixteen weeks pregnant in 2000 when she sustained a tear in her placenta that drained her womb of all amniotic fluid. Comparini's doctors told her that the child's chance of survival was nil due to the weeks left prior to birth. Comparini said she appealed to Bl. Gianna Molla asking for her intercession and was able to deliver her child in perfect health despite the lack of amniotic fluid.

Conclusion

As noted, all of the saints in this compendium lived on earth in the course of fairly recent times, indeed many of their lifetimes intersected with our own. Heroic virtue, humility, great courage and all the other aspects of holiness are, therefore, not only a characteristic of former times, but are also manifest in our own epoch. Undeniably, many of these modern saints offered the supreme witness of their lives, attesting to the truth that, even now, Christ conquers not by the blood of His enemies, but by the blood of His martyrs. When the great G.K. Chesterton was once asked why people behaved so foolishly, he replied that one does not obtain sanity until one reaches sanctity. The sanity of our saints is plainly visible in their inspirational words of wisdom and sterling pieces of advice. Their insightful and profound aphorisms provide us with a reliable guide for following Christ. The scholarly and prolific author Peter Kreeft has pointed out that just as there were more martyrs during the 20th century than during all previous centuries, there were also more recorded miracles. Many of these miracles can be attributed to the mediation of the saintly men and women described herein. May their example, wisdom, and intercession lead us, as it did them, to a closer union with Christ and His Blessed Mother, whom they served so well.

ENDNOTES

Notice on quotations in this book: The author has made every reasonable effort to cite sources for quotes not within the public domain. Admittedly, some quotes are legend and their verbatim origins have succumbed to generations of interpretation. Other quotes are attributed to the saints described in these pages, although scholarly evidence may be insufficient.

It may be necessary to insert www.http// (no semicolon) before the reference.

St. Teresa of Kolkata

a. 1. Faithandculture.com/home/2020/8/21/matthew-2540-with-st-teresa-of-calcutta.
2. Catholicculture.org/culture/library/view.cfm?recnum=185.
3. Holyheroes.com/products/glory-stories-cd-vol-4-st-teresa-of-calcutta-st-faustina-kowalska.

b. 1. Constitution of the Missionaries of Charity.
2. Exploringthesacredmystery.com/blog/mother-teresa-a-model-to-imitate.
3. Factsanddetails.com/india/Religion_Caste_Folk_Beliefs_Death/sub7_2f/entry-4163.html.

c. 1. Malcolm Muggeridge. *Something Beautiful for God*. Collins. Page 63.
2. Libquotes.com/mother-teresa/quote/lbj9j0x.
3. Worksbyfaith.org/words-of-mother-teresa-on-the-way-of-love/.

d. 1. Melanieslibrary.com/mother-teresa.
2. Fatherconlin.com/2015/07/08/something-beautiful-for-god-by-malcolm-muggeridge/.

e. 1. *Mother Teresa: A Simple Path*. Ballantine Books. Page 113.
2. Vinodvihar75.files.wordpress.com/2014/11/mother-teresa-prayer-card.pdf.

f. 1. *Mother Teresa: A Simple Path*. Ballantine Books. Page 180.

g. 1. Brian Kolodiejchuk. *Mother Teresa: Come Be My Light: The Private Writings of the Saint of Calcutta*.
2. Catholic-link.org/quotes/quote-mother-teresas-beautiful-prayer-of-total-surrender-you-are-free-then/.
3. Crossroadsinitiative.com/saints/quotes-from-blessed-mother-teresa-of-calcutta/.

h. 1. *Mother Teresa*. Catholic Truth Society. Page 47.
2. Larouchepub.com/eiw/public/1997eirv24n38-19970919/eirv24n38-19970919_058-god_bless_you_mother_teresa.pdf.

i. 1. Minimalistquotes.com/mother-teresa.
2. Catholic-link.org/quotes/st-theresa-of-calcutta-quote-spread-love-everywhere-you-go/.
3. Brainyquote.com/quotes/mother_teresa_133195.

j. 1. Getbengal.com/details/if-you-cant-feed-a-hundred-people-then-feed-just-one-tribute-to-mother-teresa.
2. Riseagainsthunger.org/quotes/cant-feed-hundred-people-feed-just-one/.
3. Dailymeditate.com/meditation-quote-70-if-you-cant-feed-a-hundred-people-feed-just-one-mother-teresa/.

k. Malcolm Muggeridge. *Something Beautiful for God*. Collins. Page 99.

l. Malcolm Muggeridge. *Something Beautiful for God*. Collins. Page 66.

m. 1. Goodreads.com/author/quotes.
2. Philosiblog.com/2012/11/01/i-have-found-the-perfect-paradox-that-if-you-love-until-it-hurts-there-can-be-no-more-hurt-only-more-love/.
3. Brainyquote.com/quotes/mother_teresa_142106.

n. *Mother Teresa*. Catholic Truth Society. Page 70.

St. Padre Pio

a. 1. Catholiccompany.com/magazine/5-quotes-padre-pio.
2. Reddit.com/r/Christianity/comments/anstdz/pray_hope_and_dont_worry_worry_is_useless_god_is/.
3. Frassatireflections.com/2019/09/23/pray-hope-and-don't-worry/.

b. 1. Pal Gallagher. *Reflecting on Padre Pio.* Loyola Press.
2. Loyolapress.com/catholic-resources/saints/saints-reflections/reflecting-on-padre-pio/.
3. Padrepiodapietrelcina.com/en/spiritual-counsels-of-padre-pio/.

c. 1. Padrepiodapietrelcina.com/en/spiritual-maxims-of-padre-pio-sayings-and-words-of-faith/.
2. Thecatholicreader.blogspot.com/2013/06/saint-padre-pio-quotes.html.
3. Goodreads.com/quotes/389836-the-life-of-a-christian-is-nothing-but-a-perpetual.

d. 1. Piercedhearts.org/theology_heart/counsels_of_%20heart/counsels_st_pio.htm.
2. Ewtn.com/catholicism/library/resignation-to-gods-will-14164.
3. Evangelizzare.org/2010/10/a-thought-for-each-day-of-the-year/.

e. 1. BJ Gonzalvo. *Lessons in Leadership from the Saints: Called to Holiness, Called to Lead.*
2. Padrepiodapietrelcina.com/en/spiritual-counsels-of-padre-pio/#:~:text=Have%20patience%20and%20persevere%20in,chosen%20God%20for%20its%20portion.

f. 1. Ncregister.com/blog/50-wise-and-wonderful-insights-from-padre-pio.
2. Piercedhearts.org/theology_heart/life_saints/padre_pio.htm.
3. Chronicallycatholic.com/2017/08/17/i-am-the-bread-of-life/.

g. 1. Lifeondoverbeach.wordpress.com/2020/04/25/padre-pio-temptations-suffered-in-patience/.
2. Ewtn.com/catholicism/library/against-temptation-14166.
3. Foundationforpriests.org/suf-quotes.

h. 1. Joseph Hollcraft. *Unleashing the Power of Intercessory Prayer.* Sophia Press.
2. Padrepiodapietrelcina.com/en/spiritual-counsels-of-padre-pio/.
3. Stalberts.org/sayings-from-padre-pio/.

i. 1. L. Bethea OP: https://www.dominicanajournal.org/a-man-for-our-time-st-padre-pio/.
2. Saintpadrepio.ca/presenters.html.
3. Quotabulary.com/famous-quotes-by-padre-pio.

j. 1. Ewtn.com/catholicism/library/padre-pio-the-priest.
2. Catholicdigest.com/from-the-magazine/quiet-moment/easier-earth-exist-without-sun/.
3. Padrepiodapietrelcina.com/en/quotes-of-padre-pio-padre-pios-words-of-faith/.

St. Edith Stein

a. 1. *The Hidden Life: Essays, Meditations, Spiritual Texts.* The Collected Works of Edith Stein, Volume IV, ed. L. Gelber, M. Linssen.
2. Asalittlechild.wordpress.com/2015/07/07/edith-stein-quote/.

b. 1. *The Hidden Life: Essays, Meditations, Spiritual Texts.* The Collected Works of Edith Stein, Volume IV, Section 3, "At the Foot of the Cross."

c. 1. AtoZ Quotes: Edith Stein.
2. Ocarm.org/EN/ITEM/2271-%20EDITH-STEIN-QUOTES.
3. Successories.com/IQUOTE/AUTHOR/35716/EDITH-STEIN-QUOTES/1.

d. 1. From a lost manuscript chapter by Eugenio Zolli.
2. Ocarm.org/en/item/2271-edith-stein-quotes.
3. Quotetab.com/QUOTES/BY-EDITH-STEIN.

e. 1. Edith Stein. "Problems of Women's Education." (1932).
2. Whatshouldireadnext.com/QUOTES/EDITH-STEIN-ALL-OUR-OWN-PRESENT-EXPERIENCES.

f. 1. EWTN.com. "Edith Stein: Daughter of Israel, Philosopher, Carmelite, Martyr."
2. Epicpew.com/11-QUOTES-OF-WISDOM-FROM-ST-EDITH-STEIN-TO-LIVE-BY/.
3. Vatican.va/NEWS_SERVICES/LITURGY/SAINTS/NS_LIT_DOC_19981011_EDITH_STEIN_EN.HTML.

g. 1. Edith Stein: The Fundamental Principles of Women's Education.
2. Whatshouldireadnext.com/QUOTES/EDITH-STEIN-BOTH-SPIRITUAL-COMPANIONSHIP-AND-SPIRITUAL.

h. 1. Catholic Saints Information. ST. Edith Stein. 14 November 2020.
2. Piercedhearts.org/THEOLOGY_HEART/LIFE_SAINTS/EDITH_STEIN.HTM
3. Inspiringquotes.us/index.php.

i. 1. St. Edith Stein (1891-1942). "Nun, Decalced Carmelite, Martyr." Vatican.va/news_services/liturgy/saints.
2. Carmelourladysdovecote.wordpress.com/2012/08/08/AUGUST-9-FEAST-OF-ST-TERESA-BENEDICTA-OF-THE-CROSS-MARTYR-EDITH-STEIN/.

j. 1. Edith Stein (2016). "Self-Portrait In Letters, 1916-1942 (The Collected Works of Edith Stein, vol. 5)", p. 283, ICS Publications.
2. Idlehearts.com/1507006/usually-one-gets-a-heavier-cross-when-one-attempts-to-get-rid-of-an-old-one.

k. 1. Edith Stein: The ethos of woman's professions (1930).
2. Carmelitenuns.uk/discernment/a-still-small-voice/a-still-small-voice-week-4-2/.
3. Quotefancy.com/quote/1427655/Edith-Stein-The-motive-principle-and-end-of-the-religious-life-is-to-make-an-absolute.

l. 1. Edsteinguild.com/FILES/ESG-CONFERENCE-DEC-3-2016-1.PDF.
2. Robert Royal. A Deeper Vision. Ignatius Press Page 98.

m. 1. Homily of John Paul II for the Canonization of Edith Stein.
2. Integratedcatholiclife.org/2015/09/sparks-truth-and-love/.

St. André Bessette

a. 1. The Story of Blessed Andre Bessette. http://semperaltius.com/Andre%20Bessett.htm.
2. D2y1pz2y630308.cloudfront.net/15495/documents/2016/11/10-Winter.pdf.

b. 1. Ann Ball. *Faces of Holiness II.* "Andre Bessette." Our Sunday Visitor Press.

c. 1. Catholicfaithonthemove.com/catholic-faith-on-the-move/2018/4/11/give-us-this-day-our-daily-bread.
2. Dailyapostle.org/HomeRead1.html.

d. 1. Innerhealingministry.org/2019/02/16/quotes-from-st-andre-bessette/.
2. D2y1pz2y630308.cloudfront.net/15495/documents/2016/11/10-Winter.pdf.

e. 1. Holycrosscongregation.org/assets/406375/quotes_from_st._andr_bessette.pdf.
2. Ewtn.com/catholicism/library/brother-andrehis-life-and-times-5288.

f. 1. Steubenvillefuel.com/2016/06/22/smallest-brushes-quote/.
2. Healthycatholics.com/?p=5763.

g. 1. Avemariapress.com/engagingfaith/brother-andre-bessette-first-holy-cross.
2. Holycrosshs.org/portal/wp-content/uploads/sites/14/2018/01/Monday-St.-Andre-Bessette.pdf.
h. 1. Slmedia.org/brotherandre.
2. Holycrosshs.org/portal/wp-content/uploads/sites/14/2018/01/Monday-St.-Andre-Bessette.pdf.
i. 1. Catholicism.org/br-andre.html.
2. Twitter.com/marysshrine/status/949651790848458754?lang=en.
j. 1. Ewtn.com/catholicism/library/a-reflection-on-st-andr-of-montreal-13323.
2. Catholicinsight.com/22432-2/.

B1. Dina Belanger

a. 1. Leveillee.net/ancestry/dinabiography.htm.
b. 1. Har22201.blogspot.com/2013/09/bienheureuse-dina-belanger.html.
2. Leveillee.net/ancestry/dinabiography.htm.
c. 1. Jehannedarc.org/divinecharity.html.
2. Piercedhearts.org/theology_heart/wisdom_heart/thoughts_of_st_dina_belanger.htm.
d. 1. Thedivinemercy.org/articles/dina-and-faustina-teachers-divine-mercy.
2. Jehannedarc.org/divinecharity.html.
e. 1. Lefleurdelystoo.blogspot.com/2009/07/qoute-of-dina-belanger-on-eucharist.html.
2. Catholicbygrace.blogspot.com/2009/09/quotes-by-blessed-dina-belanger-on-her.html.
f. 1. Catholictradition.org/Tradition/silence5.htm.
2. Contemplativeinthemud.wordpress.com/tag/dina-belanger/.

g. 1. Mysticsofthechurch.com/2010/09/blessed-dina-belanger-mother-ste-cecile.html.
    2. Mystics42.rssing.com/chan-9883335/all_p1.html.
h. 1. Ezinearticles.com/?Blessed-Dina-Belanger&id=3007599.
    2. Visionsofjesuschrist.com/weeping1416.html.
i. 1. Catholicmagazine.news/blessed-dina-belanger-jesus-and-i-are-one/.
    2. Piercedhearts.org/theology_heart/wisdom_heart/thoughts_of_st_dina_belanger.htm.
j. 1. Leveillee.net/ancestry/dinabiography.htm.

St. Josephine Bakhita

a. 1. Vatican.va/news_services/liturgy/saints/ns_lit_doc_20001001_giuseppina-bakhita_en.html.
    2. Angelusnews.com/faith/saint-of-the-day/saint-of-the-day-josephine-bakhita/.
    3. Mercymidatlantic.org/PDF/MAMBakhitaBio.pdf.
b. 1. Steubenvillefuel.com/2017/01/28/i-have-given/.
    2. Catholicdigest.com/from-the-magazine/quiet-moment/st-josephine-bakhita-i-have-given-everything/.
    3. Allsaintsheights.com/st-josephine-bakhita.
c. 1. Bigccatholics.blogspot.com/2017/02/ten-quotations-from-saint-josephine.html.
    2. Bakhita.fdcc.org/eng/bakhitas_sayings.html.
    3. Liturgicalyear.wordpress.com/2011/02/08/saint-josephine-bakhita/.
d. 1. Opusdei.org/en-ca/article/canonization-of-josephine-bakhita/.
    2. Ncronline.org/books/2021/06/woman-courage-fortitude-and-hope.
    3. Sunstar.com.ph/ampArticle/61856.
e. 1. Jean Maynard. *Josephine Bakhita*. Catholic Truth Society. Page 72.

f. 1. Jean Maynard. *Josephine Bakhita*. Catholic Truth Society. Page 68.

g. 1. Benedictdaswa.org.za/saints-martyrs/some-modern-day-saints/st-josephine-bakhita/.
2. English.op.org/godzdogz/freedom-and-slavery-st-josephine-bakhita.
3. Catholicmom.com/articles/2014/02/03/responding-to-evil-with-st-josephine-bakhita.

St. Maximillian Kolbe

a. *St. Maximilian Kolbe: Victim of the Nazis*. Catholic Truth Society. Page 14.

b. 1. Steubenvillefuel.com/2017/10/29/poison-of-indifference-quote/.
2. Catholic-link.org/saint-maximilian-kolbe/.
3. Catholicgentleman.com/2021/01/st-maximilian-kolbe-tribute-to-a-seed/.

c. 1. Integratedcatholiclife.org/2017/07/daily-catholic-quote-from-st-maximilian-kolbe-17/.
2. Young-catholics.com/3942/the-cross-is-the-school-of-love/.
3. Kolbe.ca/about/.

d. 1. Convivium.ca/voices/love-lives-through-sacrifice/.
2. Catholic-link.org/quotes/without-sacrifice-there-is-no-love-st-maximilian-kolbe/.
3. Franciscantradition.org/blog/20-maximilian-kolbe.

e. 1. Reddit.com/r/Catholicism/comments/8y19jr/if_angels_could_be_jealous_of_men_they_would_be/.
2. Aleteia.org/2017/06/01/if-angels-could-be-jealous-of-men/.
3. Ourladyofthescapular.net/first-holy-communion.

f. 1. 4catholiceducators.com/ezinekolbe.htm.
    2. Stmaximiliankolbechurch.com/about-us/biography-of-saint-maximilian.
    3. Catholicsoul.tumblr.com/post/58086568647/courage-my-sons-dont-you-see-that-we-are.

g. 1. Christiantoday.com/article/10-powerful-quotes-from-maximilian-kolbe-the-priest-who-gave-his-life-in-auschwitz/61956.htm.
    2. Crossroadsinitiative.com/media/articles/zeal-for-gods-glory-maximilian-kolbe/.

h. 1. Spxdallasschool.org/editoruploads/files/2019%20Prayers%20and%20Virtues/August_Saint_of_the_Month.pdf.
    2. Ncregister.com/tag/posture.
    3. Stjohnthebaptistontario.flocknote.com/note/8359123.

i. 1. Inspiringquotes.us/author/3698-maximilian-kolbe.
    2. Catholicgallery.org/quotes/quotes-about-mary-3/.
    3. Saintmaximiliankolbe.com/a-global-form-of-catholic-life/.

j. 1. Bustedhalo.com/dailyjolt/never-be-afraid-of-loving-the-blessed-virgin-too-much-you-can-never-love-her-more-than-jesus-did-st-maximilian-kolbe.
    2. Catholicismhastheanswer.com/saint-maximilian-mary-kolbe/.

k. 1. Atozquotes.com/quote/1198835.
    2. Quotemaster.org/q118dd20fb82c0c90e87763dbbcd53dc8.

l. 1. Airmaria.com/2013/01/19/some-eucharistic-quotes-from-st-maximilian-maria-kolbe/.
    2. Catholicfamilyvignettes.wordpress.com/2007/08/14/st-maximilian-maria-kolbe-august-14th/.
    3. Eucharisticadorationcanada.com/wp-content/uploads/2018/12/Eucharistic-Quotes-for-Bulletins.pdf.

m. 1. Goodreads.com/work/quotes/36910018-let-yourself-be-led-by-the-immaculate.
2. Corpuschristiphx.org/blog?month=201805&id= 1760515313&cat= All&pg=1&title=May+is+the+ Month+of+Mary.
3. Knightlibrary.files.wordpress.com/2017/03/she_leadeth_me_with_cover.

St. Faustina Kowalska

a. 1. *Diary of Saint Maria Faustina Kowalska*: 944.
2. Piercedhearts.org/theology_heart/wisdom_heart/faustina_prayer_merciful.

b. 1. *Diary of Saint Maria Faustina Kowalska*: 778.
2. Piercedhearts.org/theology_heart/life_saints/a_st_faustina.htm.

c. 1. *Diary of Saint Maria Faustina Kowalska*.
2. Kidadl.com/articles/st-faustina-quotes-from-the-secretary-of-divine-mercy.

d. 1. *Diary of Saint Maria Faustina Kowalska*: 46.
2. Goodreads.com/author/quotes/5497697.Maria_Faustyna_Kowalska.

e. 1. Anastpaul.com/2019/10/05/quote-s-of-the-day-5-october-st-faustina/.
2. Wisesayings.com/storm-quotes/.

f. 1. *Diary of Saint Maria Faustina Kowalska*: 82.
2. Divinemercyforamerica.org/action-plan/nurture-personal-holiness/sincere-and-frequent-confession/.

g. 1. Mercifulredeemer.org/saints/faustina-kowalska.
2. Stfaustinadiary.com/reading-assignment-32-961-1783/.

h. 1. *Diary of Saint Maria Faustina Kowalska*: 742.
2. Faustina-message.com/oredzie_ang2.htm.

i. 1. *Diary of Saint Maria Faustina Kowalska*: 267.
    2. Divinemercyforamerica.org/action-plan/nurture-personal-holiness/meditating-passion/.
j. 1. *Diary of Saint Maria Faustina Kowalska*: 150.
k. 1. *Diary of Saint Maria Faustina Kowalska*: 303.
    2. Plus.catholicmatch.com/blog/2021/04/divine-mercy-dating-relationships.
l. 1. *Diary of Saint Maria Faustina Kowalska*: 186-187.
    2. Thedivinemercy.org/articles/jesus-i-trust-you.

St. Katharine Drexel

a. 1. Catholicdigest.com/from-the-magazine/quiet-moment/st-katharine-drexel-wish-serve-god-love-neighbor-well/.
    2. Catholic-link.org/quotes/how-to-serve-god-well-according-to-st-katherine-drexel/.
    3. Stkdparish.org/welcome/.
b. 1. Saintjohninstitute.org/st-katherine-drexel/.
    2. Giveninstitute.com/st-katharine-drexel/.
    3. Catholicnewslive.com/story/614773.
c. 1. Integratedcatholiclife.org/2014/06/daily-catholic-quote-from-st-katharine-drexel-4/.
    2. Kalemati.net/tq/Faith/623172/Ours-is-the-Spirit-of-the-Eucharist-the-total-Gift-of-Self.
    3. Idlehearts.com/2098632/ours-is-the-spirit-of-the-eucharist-the-total-gift-of-self.
d. 1. Pinterest.ca/pin/551128073141503671/.
    2. Welcomehisheart.com/saint-quotes-and-feast-days-for-the-month-of-march.
    3. Catholicstoreroom.com/category/quotes/quote-topic/eucharistic-adoration/page/7/.

e. 1. Bustedhalo.com/dailyjolt/lent-2015-march-3.
2. Allsaintsheights.com/st-katharine-drexel.
3. Ignatiusloyola.org/news/memorial-of-st-katharine-drexel-1858-1955.

f. 1. Catholicgirlwellness.wordpress.com/2017/03/03/never-too-young-never-too-old/.
2. Modgnews.com/10167/uncategorized/saint-spotlight-katharine-drexel/.

g. 1. Catholicdigest.com/from-the-magazine/quiet-moment/st-katharine-drexel-kindness-is-the-natural-fruit/.
2. Livingwithchrist.us/thought_of_the_day/kindness-is-the-natural-fruit-of-goodness-of-the-heart-st-katharine-drexel/.

h. 1. Integratedcatholiclife.org/2014/03/daily-catholic-quote-from-st-katharine-drexel-3/.
2. Franciscanmedia.org/franciscan-spirit-blog/sisterhood-of-saints-katharine-drexel.
3. Knightsoftheholyeucharist.com/wp-content/uploads/2019/02/March-03-Eucharist-Download.pdf.

i. 1. Tumblr.com/tagged/katharine-drexel?sort=top.
2. Catholictothemax.com/catholic-home-decor/help-me-love-st-katharine-drexel-quote-plaque/.

j. 1. Saintkatharinedrexelshrine.com/wp-content/uploads/2019/06/printable-novena-2.pdf.
2. Tektonministries.org/seeing-a-need-and-answering-a-call/.

k. 1. Catholicism.org/katherine-drexel.html.
2. Saintjohninstitute.org/st-katherine-drexel/.

B1. Jerzy Popieluszko

a. 1. Catholiceducation.org/en/controversy/persecution/blessed-jerzy-popieluszko.html.
2. Thedialog.org/featured/our-lenten-journey-march-12-2015/.
3. Anastpaul.com/2019/10/19/quote-s-of-the-day-19-october-truth/.

b. 1. Pinterest.ca/pin/437552920048750654/.
2. Catholiceducation.org/en/controversy/persecution/blessed-jerzy-popieluszko.html.
3. Doingjourneytogether.wordpress.com/2017/08/24/messenger-of-the-truth-documentary/.

c. 1. Catholicism.org/the-touching-story-of-blessed-father-jerzy-popieluszko.html.
2. Anastpaul.com/2019/10/19/thought-for-the-day-19-october-one-doesnt-suffer-when-one-suffers-for-christ/.

d. 1. Pinterest.ca/pin/434456695299712659/.
2. Australiancatholicmums.com/truth-must-cost-us-something/#.YN8MvOhKjIU.
3. Jerzy2sainthood.com/october-8-1984-2/.

e. 1. Diocesanpriest.com/fr-jerzy-popieluszko/.
2. Anastpaul.com/2019/10/19/quote-s-of-the-day-19-october-truth/.
3. Catholicculture.org/culture/liturgicalyear/calendar/day.cfm?date=2020-10-19.

f. 1. Catholicculture.org/culture/library/view.cfm?recnum=9368.
2. Churchlifejournal.nd.edu/articles/rene-girard-and-the-present-moment/.
3. Soul-candy.info/category/october/.

g. 1. Patheos.com/blogs/christophers/2014/04/faith-freedom-nonviolence-and-truth-the-legacy-of-polish-martyr-father-jerzy-popieluszko/.
2. Evergreeneditions.com/article/Faith%2C_Freedom%2C_Nonviolence_And_Truth/1724388/211586/article.html.
3. Catholicismpure.wordpress.com/2020/10/19/father-jerzy-popieluszko-murdered-by-the-communists-19-october-1984/.
h. 1. Doingjourneytogether.wordpress.com/2017/08/24/messenger-of-the-truth-documentary/.

St. Óscar Romero

a. 1. Thecompassnews.org/2018/01/through-eyes-that-have-cried/.
2. Quotefancy.com/quote/1582637/Oscar-Romero-There-are-many-things-that-can-only-be-seen-through-eyes-that-have-cried.
b. 1. Quotemaster.org/qf46b5a6696f9791ee72675d10f60ff68.
2. Cafod.org.uk/content/download/51307/725712/version/1/COVID19%20Romero%20quotations%20activity.pdf.
3. Rcdea.org.uk/we-must-speak-for-the-voiceless-like-oscar-romero/.
c. 1. Bread.org/blog/prayer-oscar-romero.
2. Usccb.org/prayer-and-worship/prayers-and-devotions/prayers/prophets-of-a-future-not-our-own.
3. Beingchurchin21stc.wordpress.com/scripture-about-and-prayers-for-the-church/oscar-romeros-prayer/.
d. 1. Irishcatholic.com/aspire-not-to-have-more-but-to-be-more/.
2. Bcys.net/footsteps-st-oscar-romero/.
3. Sciaf.org.uk/stories/177-blessed-oscar-romero-is-to-be-canonised.
e. 1. Atozquotes.com/author/22135-Oscar_Romero.
2. Indcatholicnews.com/news/34535.

f. 1. Paulistcenter.org/the-39th-anniversary-of-the-martyrdom-of-oscar-romero-archbishop-of-san-salvador/.
2. Rcsj.org/wp-content/uploads/2020/03/e-version-LIVING-FAITH-March-22-4-Lent.pdf.
g. 1. Holyhill.ie/oscar-romero/.
2. Bustedhalo.com/dailyjolt/we-must-not-seek-the-child-jesus-in-the-pretty-figures-of-our-christmas-cribs-we-must-seek-him-among-the-undernourished-children-who-have-gone-to-bed-at-night-with-nothing-to-eat.
3. 4catholiceducators.com/ezineromero.htm.
h. 1. Goodreads.com/quotes/12247-beautiful-is-the-moment-in-which-we-understand-that.
2. Ignatiansolidarity.net/blog/2014/08/13/man-gods-microphone-12-quotes-celebrate-life-voice-oscar-romero/.
3. Albertus.edu/alumni/documents/from-romeros-homilies-speeches-and-writings.pdf.
i. 1. Onlineministries.creighton.edu/ Collaborative Ministry/Martyrs/Romero/index.html.
2. Csjcanada.org/blog/tag/Oscar+Romero.
3. Plough.com/en/topics/faith/witness/who-was-oscar-romero.
j. 1. Facpub.stjohns.edu/~ganterg/sjureview/vol4-2/05Plock.htm.
2. Ewtn.com/catholicism/library/oscar-romero-and-the-poor-5793.
k. 1. Cafod.org.uk/content/download/51307/725712/version/1/COVID19%20Romero%20quotations%20activity.pdf.
2. Sacredspace102.blogspot.com/2012/05/quotes-of-day-oscar-romero.html.
3. Inspiringquotes.us/author/8967-oscar-romero.
l. 1. Megaessays.com/viewpaper/66149.html.
2. 4catholiceducators.com/ezineromero.htm.

m. 1. Dailytheology.org/2013/03/24/oscar-romero-pray-for-us/.
2. Apprenticeshiptojesus.wordpress.com/2007/09/12/oscar-romero-quotes/.

n. 1. Bethelightofchrist.org/blogbethelight/shining-light-inspiration-after-mass-from-st-oscar-romero.
2. Brickhouseinthecity.com/saint-oscar-romero-10-quotes-from-our-newest-saint/.
3. Comonewman.org/reflect-on-the-4th-sunday-in-ordinary-time/.

St. Gianna Molla

a. 1. Grottonetwork.com/keep-the-faith/community/saint-gianna-beretta-molla/.
2. Relevantradio.com/2018/04/5-inspirational-saint-gianna-molla-quotes/.
3. All.org/st-gianna-molla-inspiring-words-to-help-build-a-culture-of-life/.

b 1. Saintgianna.org/reflectionosst.htm.
2. Bethelightofchrist.org/blogbethelight/light-from-st-gianna-beretta-molla-light-of-the-saints.
3. Steubenvillefuel.com/2016/09/19/our-body/.

c. 1. Relevantradio.com/2018/04/5-inspirational-saint-gianna-molla-quotes/.
2. Saintgianna.org/reflectionosst.htm.
3. Priestsforlife.org/library/5665-st-gianna-beretta-molla.

d. 1. Steubenvillefuel.com/2018/02/22/live-moment-by-moment-quote/.
2. Catholicreadings.org/feast-of-st-gianna-beretta-molla-daily-catholic-quotes/.
3. Ncregister.com/blog/st-gianna-s-guide-to-happiness.

e. 1. Stclare.flocknote.com/note/7018744.
2. Sths.org/wp-content/uploads/2020/05/House-of-Belisch.pdf.
3. Relevantradio.com/2018/04/5-inspirational-saint-gianna-molla-quotes/.

f. 1. Ncregister.com/blog/why-i-love-st-gianna-s-advice-to-live-holy-the-present-moment.
2. Theyoungcatholicwoman.com/archivescollection/living-holy-in-the-present-moment.
3. Catholicnewsworld.com/2015/08/catholic-quote-to-share-by-st-gianna.html.

g. 1. Stgianna.ca/wp-content/uploads/2020/05/Novena-booklet-2020-updated-for-print.pdf.
2. Timothyandtitus.wordpress.com/2011/04/29/modern-day-saint-st-gianna-beretta-molla/.
3. Priestsforlife.org/library/5665-st-gianna-beretta-molla.

h. 1. Dd2y1pz2y630308.cloudfront.net/18843/documents/2021/1/LentPaperChain.pdf.
2. Catholicvoice.org.au/7-wise-tips-from-st-gianna-molla-for-life-at-home-and-always/.
3. Thekennedyadventures.com/saints-and-scripture-sunday-st-gianna-beretta-molla/.

i. 1. Pinterest.ca/pin/285978645076401661/.
2. Littlewithgreatlove.com/st-gianna-molla/.
3. Catholicinsight.com/setting-our-faces-like-flint-and-bearing-fruit/.

j. 1. Stferd.org/st-giannas-witnesses.
2. All.org/st-gianna-molla-inspiring-words-to-help-build-a-culture-of-life/.

k. 1. Saintgianna.org/doctor.htm.
2. Aleteia.org/2020/04/28/prayer-to-dr-st-gianna-molla-for-heath-care-professionals/.

 **About Leonine Publishers**

Leonine Publishers LLC makes fine Catholic literature available to Catholics throughout the English-speaking world. Leonine Publishers offers an innovative "hybrid" approach to book publication that helps authors as well as readers. Please visit our web site at www.leoninepublishers.com to learn more about us. Browse our online bookstore to find more solid Catholic titles to uplift, challenge, and inspire.

Our patron and namesake is Pope Leo XIII, a prudent, yet uncompromising pope during the stormy years at the close of the 19th century. Please join us as we ask his intercession for our family of readers and authors.

www.leoninepublishers.com

www.ingramcontent.com/pod-product-compliance
Lightning Source LLC
Chambersburg PA
CBHW020010050426
42450CB00005B/396